I UNDERSTAND
WHAT YOU ARE
NOT SAYING

I UNDERSTAND WHAT YOU ARE NOT SAYING

Understanding How Nonverbal Communication Can
Help the Pastor in Ministry to Minister to People

MARK ALAN POPE

WESTBOW
PRESS®
A DIVISION OF THOMAS NELSON
& ZONDERVAN

WestBow Press books may be ordered through booksellers or by contacting:

WestBow Press
A Division of Thomas Nelson & Zondervan
1663 Liberty Drive
Bloomington, IN 47403
www.westbowpress.com
1 (866) 928-1240

ISBN: 978-1-9736-1529-3 (sc)
ISBN: 978-1-9736-1531-6 (hc)
ISBN: 978-1-9736-1530-9 (e)

Library of Congress Control Number: 2018900648

Scripture taken from the King James Version of the Bible.

This book is a work of non-fiction. Unless otherwise noted, the author and the publisher make no explicit guarantees as to the accuracy of the information contained in this book and in some cases, names of people and places have been altered to protect their privacy.

Print information available on the last page.

WestBow Press rev. date: 2/16/2018

ACKNOWLEDGMENTS

All glory goes to the Lord Jesus Christ as the source of my strength. Jesus has been my source of strength, wisdom, and collective peace since making Him Lord of my life some 25 years ago.

My wife Robin has been my best friend since high school, partner in life, source of encouragement, and wisdom. She has always been there for me over the last 35 years.

Roselle Lewis, my best friend and brother in-Christ, has not only been my source of confidence, but my Christian accountability partner for over 10 years.

Anyone who has been around Liberty University will also tell you how many men of faith have impacted their Christian growth and development. I too am eternally grateful for all the men (who are too numerous to mention) who have impacted my life.

PREFACE

When I completed my doctoral degree at Liberty Baptist Theological Seminary, my mentor for my thesis project recommended I write in this area for pastors. He explained that no one was writing in this area and it needed to be published as a source of help for pastors.

This book is the result of twenty-five years of law enforcement experience interviewing people (those I didn't know), thirteen and half years of pastoral communication within the church (those who I have grown to know), and a good biblical understanding of what Scripture requires of the pastor (all of who God knows).

My hope it that this book will allow you to better understand your people, understand their non-verbal cues, and determine when something is out of the norm of their behavior. When it happens, you will understand what Scripture requires. Then you can begin to help God's people.

Are you ready to take the journey in learning more? Let's begin!

CONTENTS

ILLUSTRATIONS

Figures

INTRODUCTION

Since my childhood, I have always watched people around me. Maybe you do as well. If you sit long enough in the mall and watch all the people, you really can learn something about human behavior. From the man who rolls his eyes at the thought of going into a store he is less than likely to be excited about with his wife; to the child who sees a toy in a window of a store which they *must have* as the mother continues by the window. The child's face turns from excitement to disappointment. Sometimes the funniest things in life can come from sheer observation of people. But what if you could really understand and interpret what you see?

I have been an unofficial observer in nonverbal behavior for years, but when I entered the law enforcement profession my eyes were opened to things you could learn about people from trained observation over the last 25 years. I later found out in ministry how it could help pastors to gain insight into the people they minister.

You see, in ministry, few pastors have been trained in nonverbal communication. Let's face it, our college had enough classes! But a lack of understanding of the process means we can miss clues that could help people in their time of need.

In interviews prior to the writing of this book I learned pastors do not understand nonverbal communication very well. And after a number of interactions with pastors during that period I felt the need to help understand, develop, and implement some practical techniques in the non-verbal communication process.

You see, we have to understand it is very hard at times to understand what is going inside a person by listening solely to their verbal communication alone. When signals are sent through the nonverbal communication process, we can however come close to understanding and comprehending without ever hearing a word. When we understand the nonverbal process with people and have a good basic understanding of how to successfully interact with people, it can produce potentially life-changing connections.

The Bible tells us that the ultimate goal of Christian interaction should be to produce peaceable results, with the understanding of the bond of the Holy Spirit. The writer of Hebrews gives us good advice in this interactional process, *"Follow peace with all men, and holiness, without which no man shall see the Lord"* (Hebrews 12:14, KJV).

You the pastor represent the image of God to people, even when you are unaware. Therefore you must always set the tone of the encounter with people. This will produce a peaceful interaction and maximizes the success rate of the encounter. Plus, you might be the only encounter the person may have who has a solid biblical approach to their problem. Therefore it is incredibly important you become the conduit of solid biblical counsel. In fact it is part of your pastoral calling, and I'll back that up later in the book.

It is therefore my intent in the following pages to give you a good practical understanding of nonverbal process, and cues so you may interact with people on a day-to-day basis to be effective. When you implement these nonverbal communication tools you may benefit the overall effectiveness of your ministry.

The information and sources I use in this book will bridge good secular research by seeking to explain how ministry settings and methods are different than the traditional secular institutional teachings. In addition, you will be able to establish "baseline" conditions to identify behaviors which will be noted from your previous interactions. This will allow more time to effectively *listen* to the person instead of trying to monitor behavioral patterns which are required in the interim. The ideal situation for us is to find a situation where we see indicators in God's people before they speak. Then we can begin to process good Biblical counsel and/or suggestion(s) which will help them in their time of need.

Since 55% or more of communication is nonverbal in nature, it is wise to understand its implications.[1] In other studies in recent years, the percentages are shown as high as 90% in the nonverbal communication process.[2] That is quite a lot isn't it? If you could recognize it in even 50% of interactions, would you take the risk? I know I would. Especially if the relationship of pastor/ parishioner is as important as we say it is.

There are limitations to this book though as with everything else. We will use for the purposes of this book, normal behaviors exhibited by average mental health condition(s) of the people with which you will interact. I also understand that different mental health issues will affect interaction or limit or prevent productive interaction. We will also limit the scope of research to North American societal behaviors. Cultures too affect interaction and we don't want to get too bogged down into cultural norms, nor will this book be long enough to contain them.

Finally, we cannot discount the previous knowledge of the Holy Spirit's interaction in the process as well which is to relate peace to the process. He is our Helper that lives within each believer and knows the heart we want to connect with in each situation.

I pray this book will help your understanding in this field. It is my goal to make you aware a few areas you might be blindside. I hope after reading this book you will be more interested in the interactional process and conduct research on your own to learn more in this field of study.

To God be the glory as He continues to use you for His Kingdom!

---

[1] Henry H. Calero, *The Power of Nonverbal Communication* (Redwood City, CA: Silver Lake Publishing, 2005), 5.
[2] John Maxwell, *Everyone Communicates, Few Connect* (Nashville, TN: Thomas Nelson Inc., 2010), 45.

CHAPTER ONE

A Biblical View

Nonverbal communication is seen throughout God's Word. I want to share just a few short stories to help you understand the importance of this area of study. You can take many other stories and see other different interpretations. Here is what I have noted within these few stories which relate to the topic we are now embarking.

Joseph

The book of Genesis recounts the story of a young man named Joseph who was the son of Jacob. Jacob took on many concubines and had 12 children in total. The story of Joseph I want to focus on is one of a young man's inexperience of nonverbal communication skills with his brothers from an early age. Over time in Joseph's life the Bible states the father has a distinct favor for one son:

"Now Israel loved Joseph more than all his children, because he was the son of his old age: and he made him a coat of many colors" (Gen. 37:3, KJV).

Wait a minute now; *Israel loved Joseph more than all his children*? Can you see some of the potential sibling rivalry from the beginning? I did. I think in every family, if you asked the parent and they were honest enough with you they might tell you what child was their favorite. In fact some parents (mom or dad) might tell you that one of the children which was their favorite and it might be totally opposite to the other parent.

The fact is Joseph would be used by God to take care of his family in time of distress after learning some lessons about himself and how he interacted poorly with his brothers on one listed occasion. One day Joseph is called by his father to go and check on his brothers in the field to see all was well. So he heads out to the field. Scripture does not address his previous day-to-day interaction with his brothers (who were from different mothers) although it is apparent his interaction would be significant due to family and work related ties. It is also apparent that over time his brothers didn't like him very much. The Bible tells us that Joseph's brothers even hated him over time and even made comments about even killing him. As stated in the Bible;

"And when they saw him afar off, <u>even before he came near unto them</u>, they conspired against him to slay him. And they said one to another, Behold, this <u>dreamer</u> cometh. Come now therefore, and let us slay him, and cast him into some pit, and we will say, some evil beast hath devoured him: and we shall see what will become of his dreams" (Gen. 37:18-20, KJV).

Did you note the word "*dreamer*?" That word translates "ruler" or "master" or "owner." Not a good term for your younger brother is it? Therefore one might think about this area and begin to see a pattern of resentment and sense of ownership that they felt was unwarranted.

As a young man, Joseph did not see the indicators of the malice which had been planned against him. It is clear through scripture Joseph might have avoided the consequences of his inability which would signal potential harm to him. But he was too young, naïve or careless in his ways. In fact he was just young and inexperienced in life as many of us are when we were young. We thought we knew it all! But by divine timing, grace, and provision these circumstances furthered God's plan for his future.

After Joseph was thrown into the pit, the nonverbal indicators mentioned within scripture indicate his brothers were looking for an opportunity to rid themselves of Joseph permanently. Rueben saw it and intervened.

"And Reuben heard it, and he delivered him out of their hands; and said, Let us not kill him. And Reuben said unto them, Shed no blood, but cast him into this pit that is in the wilderness, and lay no hand upon him; that he might rid him out of their hands, to deliver him to his father again."(Gen. 37:21-22, KJV)

There is no doubt Rueben was watching his brothers very carefully to determine their course of action in the life of Joseph. Then a caravan approached in the distance. Rueben knew what to look for in the brothers' nonverbal actions too. Each one of us knows our family, and knows how they react. This is what happens when you spend time with people. This is what I hope you will see in the coming pages.

"And they sat down to eat bread: and they lifted up their eyes and looked, and, behold, a company of Ishmeelites came from Gilead with their camels bearing spicery and balm and myrrh, going to carry it down to Egypt. And Judah said unto his brethren, what profit is it if we slay our brother, and conceal his blood? Come, and let us sell him to the Ishmeelites, and let not our hand be upon him; for he is our brother and our flesh. And his brethren were content. Then there passed by Midianites merchantmen; and they drew and lifted up Joseph out of the pit, and sold Joseph to the Ishmeelites for twenty pieces of silver: and they brought Joseph into Egypt" (Gen. 37: 25-28, KJV).

The phrase in verse 25 is clear the brothers were looking for an alternative and Judah had enough influence to change their mind about killing their brother. I'm not advocating his actions were correct, but it does tell us a little about influence he had over his brothers.

"They lifted their eyes and looked." (Gen. 37:25, KJV)

"And his brethren were content." (Gen. 37:27, KJV)

In the company of these brothers, all knew each other well enough, and how to nonverbally communicate. Why not get rid of the problem and make some money in the process? After selling Joseph, the Bible tells us they were content; but was everyone content? No.

Other indicators of nonverbal communicative acts are noted as the story progresses. After the sale of Joseph to the Midianites,

"And Reuben returned unto the pit; and, behold, Joseph was not in the pit; and he rent his clothes" (Gen. 37:29, KJV).

He is distraught and expresses himself in his anguish, but this isn't the only person who felt the loss. His father was grieved by the loss of his son.

The brothers conspired to let Israel know his son was killed by an "evil beast." Upon their arrival home, "... they sent the coat of many colors, and they brought it to their father; and said, this have we found: know now whether it be thy son's coat or no. And he knew it, and said it is my son's coat; an evil beast hath devoured him; Joseph is without doubt rent in pieces. And Jacob rent his clothes, and put sackcloth upon his loins, and mourned for his son many days" (Gen. 37: 32-34, KJV).

Scripture mentions two acts; one by Rueben and later Jacob of the tearing of their clothing. The process of renting clothing is a show of extreme sorrow, and anguish for the one whom died. Naturally this act of mourning occurs after the death of a loved one. The sight of these nonverbal indicators cannot be explained except as felt by the person in mourning. In many instances within their culture, words aren't spoken but conveyed their emotion by physical actions of the people in mourning. Changes in appearances are also common within all cultures in times of mourning as well. We do it in America as well, with veils over our faces and dark colors. In fact within this and other stories in Genesis are filled with death and mourning.

Later in Joseph's life (Chapter 42), Joseph by the mercy and leadership of God gains favor with Pharaoh. He becomes the governor of the controlling corn crop in Egypt. Jacob realizes a famine has come upon the land and sends his sons to purchase corn in Egypt. By this time Joseph (now in Egypt) learned the value of nonverbal communication. He changed his appearance and used it for his own purposes. And it only took changing a few things in the nonverbal realm;

"And Joseph saw his brethren, and he knew them, but made himself strange unto them, and spake roughly unto them; and he said unto them, whence come ye? And they said, from the land of Canaan to buy food" (Gen. 42:7, KJV).

Joseph changed his appearance to the brothers who never recognized him at this point. The brothers were now intimidated by him by his appearance and harshness spoken to them by this stranger. Joseph used the changes in his appearance to obtain a desired result to demonstrate his power appointed by Pharaoh and authority over them (not to mention his probable anger from the past). Clothing has a distinct characteristic in the way we see people each day. It fooled his brothers. And it fools a lot of people today by what we see others wear. Let that settle for a minute as you think about how you might have judged someone in the past based on their clothing appearance.

It is clear Joseph was young and uninformed about nonverbal communication. He never saw the dangers early in his own life. As a result, he was placed into bondage and learned some hard lessons as God took him on the journey of a lifetime. It took years for him to learn the value of understanding and using nonverbal communication to affect his life with positive results. Let's obviously not discount the divine sovereignty of God in his entire life as well. But as a result of his learning, God used this circumstance in Joseph's life. He emerged from a slave to a governor over Pharaoh's land. During this famine he saved the rest of his family and countless others. Nevertheless, he used nonverbal communication to obtain some desired results.

Jesus

A second observation comes from the life of Jesus who knows the heart of every man. Jesus is the expert in recognizing nonverbal indicators. He is God! In the book of Mark a story is told of a crippled man healed after being lowered from a roof which was disassembled to lower him right where Jesus stood. After the miracle of healing occurred, Mark makes an observation in the change of behaviors of the scribes,

"But there were certain of the scribes sitting there, and reasoning in their hearts." (Mark. 2:6, KJV).

The Lord knows the thoughts of every man though. It is interesting to note Mark's comment on the change of the scribes' demeanor as opposed to everyone in the room who just witnessed a miracle. They might have been the only ones in the room who weren't exactly excited by what they just saw.

The commentator A. T. Robertson has an interesting comment on this passage. He states;

> "Another of Mark's pictures through Peter's eyes: These scribes were there to cause trouble, to pick flaws in the teaching and conduct of Jesus. His popularity and power had aroused their jealousy. There is no evidence that they spoke aloud the murmur in their hearts, "within themselves." It was not necessary, for their looks gave them away and Jesus knew their thoughts and perceived their reasoning."[3]

Scripture further asserts the conclusion of Robertson by stating;

> "And immediately when Jesus perceived in his spirit that they so <u>reasoned</u> within themselves, he said unto them, why reason ye these things in your hearts?"(Mark. 2:8, KJV).

The word *"reasoning"* here means *to debate (internally) or to create a dialog in one's heart.* It is apparent that Jesus knew the heart of every man in the room. It is also noted that the reasoning was apparent even to Jesus in reading their behavior by trying to stir the pot. He could see into the hearts of those men. Their thoughts and nonverbal actions gave them away and He called them out.

Does that really happen? Can our *looks* give us away? Absolutely! Think of that time when you said something stupid and remembered it was something you couldn't take back. Now think about the time you said something that you didn't even know would come out of your mouth and then felt like a fool. Imagine what your *own* face said nonverbally and your reaction to your own statement? Imagine what others thought when they

---

[3] A. T. Robertson, *Word Pictures in the New Testament* (Nashville, TN: Broadman Press, 1930), 268.

saw it? Do you think that might make us a little more conscious about the things we say in the future? Probably not, because we are so blindside to our own weaknesses we never notice it.

On an unrelated note, I laughingly think of what it must have been like to be the perfect kid in the family. I know I wasn't that one. Can you imagine what it was like to have your brother being Jesus? What kind of sibling rivalry must have gone on in that house? Having the perfect kid? Never disobeying his parents or sinning against them or others? Even his parents couldn't stand up to that! And all of the siblings living with Jesus each day still did not believe in Him. They never understood what His life was all about. In fact, scripture mentions that His own brothers thought he had been out in the sun for too long once in scripture;

"For neither did his brethren believe in him." (John 7:5, KJV)

The Repentant Woman

A third observation from scripture reveals a story from the book of Luke, chapter 7 of the woman whom was forgiven by Jesus:

"And, behold, a woman in the city, which was a sinner, when she knew that Jesus sat at meat in the Pharisee's house, brought an alabaster box of ointment, And stood at his feet behind him weeping, and began to wash his feet with tears, and did wipe them with the hairs of her head, and kissed his feet, and anointed them with the ointment. Now when the Pharisee which had bidden him saw it, he spake within himself, saying, This man, if he were a prophet, would have known who and what manner of woman this is that toucheth him: for she is a sinner." (Luke 7:37-39, KJV)

How this woman entered into this home without being a burglar is a strange Middle Eastern custom. This custom allowed strangers into a house as an uninvited guest seeking a gift as a beggar. This woman knew her condition in sin and offered her most valued possession (an alabaster box of ointment) in an act of genuine repentance to Jesus. She offered no conversation to Jesus when she stood at his feet weeping at her sin and showing the sincerity of her repentance. Her tears washed His feet and her hair dried them. This constituted her nonverbal act of repentance. The kissing of His feet and anointing of oil were of an act of worship for the forgiveness. In fact, there are no recorded Scripture words spoken by this woman. It was only the act of humility which Jesus forgave her. This too is a nonverbal act.

Scripture further asserts the Pharisee in Luke chapter 7 invited Jesus to his home had inner thoughts as well.

"Now when the Pharisee which had bidden him saw it, <u>he spake within himself</u>, saying, this man, if he were a prophet, would have known who and what manner of woman this is that toucheth him: for she is a sinner." (Luke 7:39, KJV)

"He spake within himself" was the inner dialog of this man's thoughts. But recognize this, his demeanor gave him away. You can bet that there was a look of disgust or a smirk which gave him readily away. None of us realize half of the time what we really are saying nonverbally, but Jesus recognized the attitude and demeanor of the Pharisee. He even challenged his inner thoughts and outward nonverbal expression by calling him out. His behavior was obviously apparent to the Savior and maybe anyone else who might have been looking at him during that time. Jesus being omniscient used this example to show Simon (the Pharisee) his previous knowledge of the woman and used it in a teachable way to share with him his true motive.

A Quick Wrap Up

It is because of scriptures mentioned above we understand the implications of nonverbal communication and the spiritual implications which affect spirit-filled people. These people in the Bible did not discover where they fell short and paid the price in their ignorance in many cases. Jesus knowing the hearts of all men knew their needs was more spiritual in nature than just physical. This is why we need to understand the crucial connection that needs to be made in both. I heard this statement a while ago and it is so true: "At the heart of every issue lies a spiritual problem."

Because of the Holy Spirit's presence within the life of the believer, we must not only establish what is not being said but understand the need to *connect* with people in the spiritual realm. For this purpose I believe that the knowledge of scripture is critical for us to understand God's people. Throughout this book I will be bridging many different fields of study in nonverbal communication. Then I will bring them all together to assert the need for more than just what society has to offer. This will be presented in a way we can use to connect with people.

We have the Spirit of God who lives within us. He lives within believers and knows us better to our core than anyone ever could. Every one of us has a certain amount that we share with people to a certain extent. The more closely we grow and know a person the more we share. I don't think that there is one person on this earth to whom we share everything. You are a rare breed if so. The only person who knows deep and sometimes dark things about us is God - Almighty. To discount Him in the nonverbal communication process would not only insult Him, but incomplete our learning!

CHAPTER TWO

A Basic Understanding of the Nonverbal Communication Process

Some Basic Definitions

At this point within the book I think it is necessary to provide the basics of the nonverbal process. To skip this part would negate nearly all we need to learn concerning the process and why the nonverbal communication process is so important in human interaction. So for the purposes of this chapter we need to look at some facts and research available on the topic. This might be a little dry for some of you at times. If you stick with it though, you will find a wealth of information that will help you in the future. So find a file drawer in your mind and prepare to gather some good information for the future. It will pay off, trust me!

When understanding this topic within the context of pastoral counseling, it is important that we look at several bodies of research that have been completed. For this reason a biblical approach to pastoring and specifically nonverbal communication is going to be reviewed. This is from insights and guidelines of respected pastoral counselors and biblical research completed in the field.

Another area that we need to study from outside the realm of pastoring which is foundational to understanding is secular nonverbal communication itself. We will gain special insight from secular bodies of knowledge as we apply these in the pastor / parishioner interaction. So let's begin with some definitions of what nonverbal communication is and is not.

Nonverbal communication is defined by Martin Remland as;

"Communication without words."[4] While this definition is one sentence, he also gives a little more insight in the next statement:

> "This is the most common definition, and the one generally regarded as reasonable. However, it is much easier to say that nonverbal communication is communication without words than it is to apply the definition to the various signals usually regarded as nonverbal. In short, are all nonverbal signal systems are truly communication codes that do not contain words."[5]

Remland conveys the thought that nonverbal communication is much more than one can imagine since signal systems can be varied in nature. These signal systems must be understood from the onset to begin or enhance the communication process. He states nonverbal communication is more of what is *not* spoken than said; hence the title of this book. So we could simply say that nonverbal communication is what is not said.

Judee Burgoon, Laura Guerrero and Kory Floyd define nonverbal communication as similar to the term communication but with a few caveats. They state:

> "Within the domain of human communication, most scholars agree that communication refers to the process of creating meanings between senders and receivers through the exchange of signs and symbols. Messages originate as sender cognitions that are encoded (transformed into signals) through commonly understood codes and decoded by receivers (the signals must be recognized, interpreted, and evaluated). Formal languages, American Sign

---

[4] Martin S. Remland, *Nonverbal Communication in Everyday Life* (Boston, MA: Houghton Mifflin Company, 2003), 19.
[5] Ibid, 19.

Language and Morse code also meet these requirements. Nonverbal codes, then, must include the same properties."[6]

In the nonverbal realm they further assert:

"In short, the passive or involuntary displays of cues that an observer might want to interpret should be treated only as information or behavior and not specifically as communication. It is given off rather than given. To be communication, the behavior must be volitional and other-directed (targeted to a receiver or receivers)."[7]

This type of nonverbal communicators is expressed by a sender so that it emanates from the person with *how* it is being expressed. Any person who has observed American Sign Language (ASL) understands the language can be used explicitly to relay strong feelings to the recipient. These are also presented through deeply expressive nonverbal communicators while using ASL language. Anyone who has seen the passion and eagerness with any deaf person communicating in ASL knows this to be true. Many times the ASL communication process seems to be exaggerated when communicating. This is used as signals which convey sincerity, passion, and or excitement many times. Sometimes they are even more exaggerated with those whom the relationship is more intimate. Remember this, the more intimate the relationship the more we share. The more we share the truer and passionate our expressions become.

My hometown of St. Augustine, Florida has one of the top Deaf and Blind Schools (Florida School for the Deaf and Blind or FSDB, established in 1885) within the United States of America. Living in this city has allowed me to witness these interactions on a weekly basis. In my past profession in law enforcement have interviewed people from the deaf community and found these statements to be true. Some I interviewed seemed to be overly

---

[6] Judee K. Burgoon, Laura Guerrero, and Kory Floyd, *Nonverbal Communication* (Boston, MA: Pearson Education Inc., 2010), 12.
[7] Ibid, 13.

expressive because of the passionate responses of innocence or denial. I also have friends from the deaf community and found these factors to be true as well. There is a true sense from this community to be *understood* as well as heard. Therefore the interactions are sometimes very passionate as they try very hard to be *understood*.

Nonverbal communication is also understood by certain norms within society and their acceptance within society. These relate information which is more accurately understood by the recipient because of the former understandings, upbringing, or cultural acceptances. Other non-volitional information is sent or given off without the sender understanding their actions but are observed by the receiver. Some of these subtle indicators (even such cases as pupil dilation) cannot be faked with enough consistency since most of the time it is unknown or involuntary in nature.

For instance, if a person who is trying to hide their intoxication cannot hide the fact the pupil dilation is present. It doesn't work when they are trying to convince a person that there is nothing wrong (not to mention their smelly breath). The eyes unfortunately show the evidence and in many cases, so do the mouth or skin which permeates it. We have all seen it before and know what it looks like.

Mark Knapp and Judith Hall define nonverbal communication as; "Communication effected by means other than words, assuming words are the verbal element." Furthermore they assert;

> "Like most definitions, this one is generally useful, but it does not account adequately for the complexity of this phenomenon. As long as we understand and appreciate the listed here, this broad definition should serve us well. First we need to understand that separating verbal and nonverbal behavior into two separate and distinct categories is virtually impossible... we need to understand that our definition does not indicate whether the phrase by means other than words refers to the type of signal produced---that is its encoding---or to the perceiver's code for interpreting the symbol, its decoding. Generally, when

people refer to nonverbal behavior, they are talking about the signals produced, or encoded, to which meaning will be attributed, not the process of attributing meaning."[8]

These meanings are understood when they are produced within societal acceptances and/or understanding from the past. These include signals which are known by the recipient when communicating in the nonverbal realm. It is then up to the recipient to determine or *decode* the meaning of the sender's *encoding* to which meaning will be attributed. Then, an understanding can be obtained by the recipient.

Henry Calero states his understanding of nonverbal communication in a little more practical term:

> "Whenever we perceive information that is not written or spoken, we comprehend something that is nonverbal. Humans have the capability of receiving information besides what is written or spoken. Our senses of touch, taste, seeing, hearing, smells, signs, symbols, colors, facial expressions, gestures, postures, and intuition area the primary sources of the nonverbal messages we receive. It is a silent language not formally taught, and which has existed before the language was invented."[9]

Calero helps us understand how much everyone is required to observe and process the interactional process. He also expresses how many different types of information and signals can be conveyed at one time. He asserts from the very beginning of life we begin to understand these signals as a baby can understand the facial expressions of their mother. Burgoon, Guerrero and Floyd also support this thought within their research. When all these factors come together for common understanding we can have a good understanding of what is being communicated. Since all our

---

[8] Mark L. Knapp and Judith Hall, *Nonverbal Communication*, 1.
[9] Henry Calero, *The Power of Nonverbal Communication*, 1.

senses are needed in nonverbal communication, all of us would do well to understand the implications and decoding of the multitude of senses throughout the process. To negate one part of the nonverbal process could potentially cause a misunderstanding. This disables the person's ability to connect and understand what is being conveyed. It also limits the receiver in the full meaning of what the sender may be trying to express. When this happens this creates frustration on the part of each person leading to a breakdown in communication.

Blake Neff explains his understanding of nonverbal communication as:

> "Any time two people are in proximity messages are being sent. Any behavior can communicate as long as another person is involved in the communication event and that person assigns a meaning to the message. All behavior in an interactional setting communicates; therefore, if you are interacting with another person, all your behavior communicates something."[10]

Neff mentions the need for the understanding that no matter what one might think, messages are being sent whether each person realizes it or not. As perceptive beings, we are consistently sending messages when another is observing us. When these messages are sent, the other person will assign a meaning to the signal(s) in the communication process. It is also clear from Neff the level of proximity determines the level of interaction, comfort in the relationship, or orientation to the other person. We will cover this phenomenon later in the area of proximity and space when we arrive at that chapter. It is also interesting how we as Americans have a comfort space we assign through the different levels of our relationship with others.

Other effects which are relevant during the process will constitute the various expressions of nonverbal communication. Each is equally important if you want to become effective in the nonverbal process. At

---

[10] Blake Neff, *A Pastors Guide to Interpersonal Communication* (Binghamton, NY. Haworth Pastoral Press. 2006), 24.

this point I want to break down these into the following categories for easy identification and understanding in this chapter and the following.

The Surroundings of the Individual (The Place around You)

This section is where it really gets interesting though. When it comes to lighting, temperature, environment, and others is where few people spend any time and research. Its implications to interaction are huge and can make a big difference in whether you *connect* or just *communicate*. Do you ever ask yourself why certain restaurants, schools, work areas lay out the design, lighting, and colors upon their walls? It's all for a reason and has been well studied to improve the results for success.

So let's deal with some perceptions in environment, light, temperature, noise, color, and objects. Each one of us encompass different interactions each day such as noise, changes in lighting whether outside or indoors, hot or cold conditions, humidity or dry conditions, and another multitude of factors which affect interaction.

Of course you are aware that there are certain times of the day when some of us are more sluggish or alert to interaction. Let's just be honest; sometimes we just don't feel like it. Other times we do. Maybe these are caused by sight related conditions or observances which cause certain reinforcement or distractions (maybe a glaring sun through a window), and/or through previous positive or negative experiences (maybe a bad experience in that location). A lot of these conditions can affect behavior or interaction. Remember, a little change can affect our interaction either for the good or bad.

Let me prove what I'm saying. When I was in my 20's, I remember going into a restaurant and noticing lower lighting and not having a problem reading the menu. I thought it was pretty cool at the time because it was a cozy environment. Now in my 50's, I find myself slightly bothered by having to take my glasses out to read the menu because of the lower lighting. It didn't bother me twenty years ago. Now I notice that over the day my eyes get more tired and I'm slightly inconvenienced with digging out my glasses. I recognize why the restaurant does this though.

Here are a few factors to consider in the world around you and why sometimes they are the way they are:

1. Environment - certain types of environment will dictate the behavior of the person where they are located. These conditions and characteristics are part of our surroundings which are physical in nature and/ or placed there for specific purposes to assist in the interaction. Burgoon, Guerrero and Floyd in their book state;

    > "We really don't acquire the environmental code in any direct sense. Rather we acquire reactions to the environment, by learning (a) that we can interpret meaning from the environment; (b) that certain contexts prompt different kinds of interaction; and, (c) that certain environment cues imply sets of rules and guides for behavior."[11]

Isn't it interesting to note how a person can use different types of environments to determine standards of behavior and /or rules? These environments in which we communicate may be conducive for the interaction or set a tone for the environment. This may lead you to select an area in the future where you might interact in an environment which can control or flourish the interactional process. This might even be whether you decide to sit behind a desk, which might convey a formal or authorative style of interaction. When you use this, expect that this conveys to the person sitting across from the person at the desk that other party will remain the authority in the interaction. This sets the tone that there might not be too much flexibility at for the person on the other side of the desk that time. On the other hand, you might take a seat near the person to convey a more personal setting in which can convey compassion or personal interest and care for the person. Either way, we decide what

---

[11] Burgoon, Guerrero, and Floyd, *Nonverbal Communication*, 172.

will have an effect on the person from the onset of the interaction and it sets the tone from the onset.

If you have ever sat in an office across from the other person behind the desk, you sometimes felt like you were in trouble (and if you were like me, you probably were). This makes the interactional process more structured. Perhaps the person behind the desk did not even realize they had diminished the potential for interaction. This is because they didn't realize the person on the other side was "on-guard" from the onset. They were always wondering what was going to happen to them rather than listen to the conversation coming out of the other parties' mouth.

2. Light - Light can be used for certain situations which can control or determine the purpose of the meeting. Lower light levels many times are used for the purpose of social interactions, where higher levels of light set a task oriented tone. Burgoon, Guerrero and Floyd further confirm this by saying; "This is why you often find lower levels of lighting in a restaurant or bar than in an office or classroom."[12]

By you determining the level of interaction, whether socially or for a task related purpose, you can allow the person with whom you interact to feel the most comfortable and more agreeable. This may later provide personal disclosure where other highly lit areas might not have accomplished this goal. Strange how a little light changes things isn't it? This is why many coffee shops, restaurants, and even homes are not brightly lit. I should also strongly say that these lower light conditions can also be detrimental to the one who may be interacting with person(s) of the opposite sex. You might want to reconsider this setting. The tone of these types of settings may make the opposite sex feel uncomfortable or a little too intimate. There are also many other things that should be considered as well. Don't fall into a trap because you are not prepared. Falls within pastors lives were never planned from the onset.

On the other hand, tones can be set for accomplishing set goals by

---

[12] Ibid, 179.

allowing the maximum light in the area which provides better concentration for task related working topics. This helps any person in the area to have the maximum amount of light to allow better concentration on the task such as meetings, stores, etc. This is why schools and classrooms are often brightly lit which allows for maximum concentration on the desired result. Plus, as you get older and need glasses, no one has to tell you how much more light helps you focus and not strain to read.

In correctional institution settings, the lighting is bright inside the institutional walls, but not for the reason you might think. The reason for the maximum lighting is for the purpose of safety and observation by officers within the facility, not task related concentration of the inmates. These higher lit areas allow maximum observation for the safety for the inmates and staff, while providing the ultimate goal; safety and security. Besides, who wants the inmates having an environment where they can set to a task of how to create mischief or escape?

3. Temperature - Temperature has an impact on the mood of the person who we will be interacting as well. Knapp and Hall observe in their book, *Nonverbal Communication is Human Interaction*;

    "Temperature changes for lengthy times, season changes and barometric pressures all affect the person as well. Since the body is made up of 80% water with 20% solid, these changes affect the person's physical body. While some parts of weather, humidity, barometric pressure change the person who may feel better, long periods of rain and cold can increase the chances for depression. Some of the ways in which our behavior varies with the seasons include the following:"[13]

    a. Suicide rates and admissions to the public mental health hospitals rise dramatically in the spring and peak in the summer.

---

[13] Knapp and Hall, *Nonverbal Communication is Human Interaction*, 107.

b. College students tend to break up with their dating partners at the beginnings and endings of semesters (May/June, August/ September, or December/ January).

c. During the summer, people tend to see their friends more often.

d. During the summer, crimes of assault and rape increase.

e. From July to November, people tend to report less happiness but more activity and less boredom.

A person who sits in your auditorium, church, public venue, etc. which is somewhat warm might find themselves getting sleepy or lethargic. On the other hand, a place which is overly cool might cause irritation and inability to concentrate on the message. This is because the person's concentration is on staying warm. These two different environments can cause all types of responses from people. This is why you as a leader need to determine the maximum level of comfort for those who will attend. It may determine whether someone is tuning in or not. If you have ever sat in another church, many times it has been too cold or too warm. Most of your time was spent thinking of how cold or hot it may be and not really paying attention to the sermon. It doesn't even matter how hard the speaker is trying to connect or the Holy Spirit to convict and convince! I have been in churches so cold that I wonder if we froze the Holy Spirit out of the building! I say this in jest, but it really does make a difference in the receptivity level of those who are in our buildings.

4. Noise - Burgoon, Guerrero, and Floyd ask a really good question regarding noise in their book, *Nonverbal Communication*; "But what precisely is noise? Holahan (1982) suggested that noise is any sound which the listener doesn't want to hear. Noise, therefore, isn't just sound; instead it is sound that one finds psychologically aversive. Rap

music is art to some and noise to others; likewise, some people enjoy opera and others think of it as noise."[14]

The level of noise will obviously determine the interaction's success as well. A quiet area might provide a good environment, while too much silence could interfere with the person's ability to disclose. It might be they don't want outsiders to hear them. On the other hand, too much noise creates irritation by both the sender and receiver of the conversation. This makes the entire sending and receiving process difficult. It also affects the interpretation of the message which is trying to be sent. This can lead to problems in the communication process from the onset. The last thing we want to do is to fail from the beginning.

If you have ever been into a movie theater you know quickly when the volume is also too loud to handle. It creates trouble on the concentration rate of what is being viewed. In other words, turning up the volume to a movie doesn't make it any better or impactful. Sometimes it's just louder and more irritating. All of us know how irritating it is to watch our favorite television show and then commercials between are so loud. The sponsors might do this because many people walk away from the television. The sponsors want to make sure you hear their message so they make sure you can. I mute mine.

How about this? Have you ever sat in traffic and someone has their bass cranked up to eleven? Isn't it irritating? While you sit as a prisoner until the next light with the bolts in your car slowly rattling loose every minute, you slowly get more irritated. In meantime, they may enjoy impressing their friends or maybe just going deaf! Of course I'm joking here (or maybe not) but you understand what I am trying to say. These conditions can even change our mood and affect the next interaction. Hopefully, it is not while the light is still red whereby you blow up on the person. This is our natural reaction many times to ill perceived noise. Wait until the light has changed to green, move away from the noise, and be free!

---

[14] Burgoon, Guerrero, and Floyd, *Nonverbal Communication*, 181.

5. Color - Burgoon, Guerrero, Floyd, Knapp and Hall refer to instances of color which are used within inmate correctional settings as well to adjust behavior. They note the importance of color within these types of settings. Although it is highly successful in some settings, while others had considerable problems with mischief while adjusting or modifying color schemes. In fact psychologists are hired to give input into these color schemes. Knapp and Hall note from their studies that this is still a work in progress though:

> "Nevertheless, the preceding reports show how various institutions have tried with mixed results, to apply the findings from color research to affect the nature of human interaction in certain environments."[15]

Back in early 1986, I was a young correctional officer working at a county jail which was built in 1956. The old jail was a dark and cold environment. It even had dark colored walls. The original steel bars were in the cell areas like you see in the movies. The new county jail was going to be completed in mid-1986. We were getting ready to move the inmates into the new facility within a few months. Just a few months before the new building opened we heard the Florida Department of Corrections delayed the transition of moving the inmates. They explained that the paint color scheme had not been selected for the new County Jail and therefore prevented the transition. The color designation for each area of confinement, from nonviolent offenders to violent was still being considered. Each needed differing paint color schemes within the respective detention cells. In fact, some of the visitation areas were also different paint color schemes. The purpose was to influence the quality of the visits. So you see, color really does make a difference and it is studied by experts to determine outcomes of behavior.

Colors are also used in numerous settings to determine the maximum amount of retention and reception in the learning environment as well.

---

[15] Knapp and Hall, *Nonverbal Communication in Human Interaction*, 115.

Knapp and Hall state the importance of the use of colors within a learning environment and how they influence the learning process:

> "Colors are also believed to influence student learning. Colors which will facilitate, or at least not impede, learning are always a concern during classroom construction."[16]

Learning institutions also take the time to consider the colors which will be selected for the purpose of facilitating the learning process. Those who take this time should notice a better level of retention and reception. In fact, some churches might take a hint from these settings to determine a color scheme which might help differentiate what is considered for offices, meeting rooms, and obviously the sanctuary. It might even make a difference in the interactional level of persons who attend the church.

In the area of clothing, color is also used to affect the interactional process. For instance, I have noted over the years how business executives, all the way to the President of the United States use the color of shirts and ties to covey hidden messages. In fact, many times colored ties are preselected for the person prior to the presentation. These colors indicate the overall tone of the message which is being nonverbally communicated. The color red and black exhibits power and control; blue and green to convey calm and compassion; while white to purity. These colors are no accident when used by these people and are used for specific purposes. They convey intended messages to the audience nonverbally. Normally the common observer assigns meaning to it because of societal norms associated with the particular color.

So the next times you see someone's color of tie in your environment, you might consider what is being conveyed and see if your conclusion may be correct. You might see the color and realize later the color of the garment worn gave your insight into the message to come. The experts take the time to consider these factors. But take into consideration that not *everyone* who puts on a tie does it with any knowledge of what they are doing or purpose

---

[16] Ibid, 115.

at that time. They might just like the way it matches their outfit. This is why it is important as we go along to understand how to look at the entire picture and not assign meaning to one nonverbal signal.

Color has specific influence on people in a number of ways as well. Some colors appeal more to some than others. Some colors strike people in different ways. Knapp and Hall found this out in a survey they conducted upon a group of persons.

They provide a chart from Wexner (1954) in which 8 colors and 11 mood-tones were presented to 94 research participants:[17] These results are interesting to note how societal norms are already inclusive into our society without us ever noticing. These results were from average people who had not been schooled in the purpose of each color and their significance assigned of the research.

Mood-Tone	Color	Number of Times Chosen
Exciting/ Stimulating	Red	61
Secure/ Comfortable	Blue	41
Distressed/ Disturbed/ Upset	Orange	34
Tender/ Soothing	Blue	41
Protective/ Defending	Red	21
	Brown	17
	Blue	15
	Black	15
	Purple	14
Despondent/ Dejected/ Unhappy/ Melancholy	Black	25
	Brown	25
Calm/ Peaceful/ Serene	Blue	38
	Green	31
Dignified/ Stately	Purple	45
Cheerful/ Jovial/ Joyful	Yellow	40
Defiant/ Contrary/ Hostile	Red	23
	Orange	21
	Black	18
Powerful/ Strong/ Masterful	Black	48

Source: Data from Mark Knapp and Judith Hall, *Nonverbal Communication in Human Interaction* (Boston, MA: Wadsworth Cengage Learning, 2010), table 1.

Table 1: Colors Associated With Moods

---

[17] Ibid, 114.

This chart furnished by Knapp and Hall will help you understand the colors associated with moods and how they were perceived by the respondents. The second column lists the colors which were used in the study. The third column lists how many times each color were associated with the mood or tone. This shows the level of understanding by different persons who were surveyed and how each color was perceived. One thing that stands clear though; it is the clear understanding that most people have about what are considered "power colors." It is also interesting how these colors have made their way into the lives of the persons interviewed without any previous interaction or influence from the onset of the survey. It proves how societal norms have entered into our society and many from an early age.

6. Objects - The placement of objects within any setting will give you an idea on what type of interaction you want to engage. When objects are selected in the environment of the proposed interaction, careful consideration should be given to how objects are placed. These placements can affect the interaction. Again, small changes affect interaction.

   Knapp and Hall note:

   > "Several studies have shown that the placement of partition, chairs, desks, or sofas in a room can encourage or discourage interaction. Sociofugal arrangements direct people away from each other (just like a centrifuge spins particles away from one another); sociopetal arrangements bring people together."[18]

Knapp and Hall tell us how one arrangement can be used for separating people in the way things are located, while others for flourishing and enhancing. These items are placed in a relational pattern which will make the area conducive for interaction. This should give good practical advice to

---

[18] Ibid, 177.

someone who remains behind his desk with someone who seeks his counsel on the other side of the desk. By doing so, the person behind the desk directs the person away from him. This also influences or changes the appearance to an authoritative figure instead of one who wants to be received as caring and compassionate. The office needs to be arranged in such a way which would provide a good environment for flourishing the interaction, if this is the intention. So in short, if you want a good interaction where you seek to connect with the person as caring and compassionate then get out from behind the desk and sit next to them. Not really hard is it? How many of us have forgotten to do so though. Now if you want to let the person know you are in charge and are disciplining them (and want them to know who is in charge) then remain behind the desk. This should give the person on the other side of the desk the nonverbal picture of the school principle behind his desk. Remember, that student is not listening but waiting for the discipline to be handed out. However, the pastor who wants to have the mindset of Jesus knows he must sit as Jesus did, *with the person*. We are pastors and leaders, not school principals no matter how much people act like children some times. Leaders interact with people, manager's process data and policies.

Even in my own encounters with pastors in the past, I have seen mistakes when sitting and talking with them. I don't think that every pastor was aware of their body language communication to the other person. It again serves to prove the point of the pastor's awareness in these times that he may be communicating something he never intended when meeting with someone. Since messages are sent and received as previously stated, you would be wise to consider potential physical barriers to communication. We never know when one thing out of place might be received as a hostile message to the one we are trying to connect. These things are not always easy to change. This is because we get into the same way of doing things over the years and change is hard for all of us. Changing the environment is hard sometimes and not always practical for us, but it could lead to greater success in interaction.

Consider this practical point as well from Knapp and Hall; how a person may place a drink on a break room table to encourage interaction with the person it is placed beside. This shows the interest by the person whom it may be placed by in proximity to that person. It also may reserve the space where they want to sit. This sends a hidden message they want to interact with that person. If the person moves or leaves at that time it's pretty obvious what the other person at the table thought at that moment. On the other hand, that same drink can be placed on an empty table which sends a signal to people around them that they may want personal privacy instead of interaction with anyone else; hence becoming solely territorial to that area. The person could also use items to spread out on the table indicating his desire to be alone or unbothered. Back years ago, I used to have a coworker who would spread his lunch, book, and other items out on one table as to take over the whole table. This was so that no one would bother him. If someone would approach the table, he would immediately pick up his book and begin reading. He sent a signal that he did not desire any company or conversation. Thereby he created a barrier to communication by holding the book up nonverbally communicating his will to be alone and unbothered.

Isn't it funny how strange we all act at different times depending on our moods and how we feel on a particular day? Try this experiment: Do the same thing to someone else sometime and see how they react to your barrier. Then watch them either get up and move somewhere else or answer your request nonverbally by remaining silent at the table.

CHAPTER THREE

Physical Characteristics
(The Person in Front of You)

In this section, let's talk about self-esteem, physical characteristics (to include body shape, face, color, smell, hair, and clothing) by differing personality types. We should understand that we send hidden messages through these. Our physical body characteristics can determine an initial response to another as relational, on the other hand as too casual or unconcerned. Hair, color, and smell can appeal or offend our fellow human based upon one's presence or preference. Since these standards or perceptions in our culture determine the way in which we interact with people we must be aware of the physical characteristics that permeate the culture we live. Therefore it is important for us to understand these characteristics and how they affect the interactional process. To provide a simple understanding of these areas, let's look at some simple definitions so we can better understand this area:

1. Self-Esteem - Women who seek acceptance within society may find themselves using clothing, cosmetics, or colognes to make themselves more attractive to the person they will be interacting. In some cases this is not always true but it can be a good indicator for us to observe when these characteristics change. This is especially true when the change is a departure or opposite of their previous behavior. These changes are triggered during times of stress or crisis when the norm is somehow out of balance. None of us like getting older with the pains and deteriorations that come with the aging process but Knapp and

Hall tell us how the aging process has a lot to do with how we look at ourselves:

"Greater attractiveness for those between the ages of 40 and 60 was perceived as most beneficial for masking the aging process and improving one's physical and mental health. And training in the use of cosmetics for elderly women has reportedly had a positive effect on their self-image…"

They further comment,

"Men, similarly experience the same in which "they think better of themselves when they feel attractive."[19]

Men as much as many will deny in secret, too struggle with the aging process at times. This is why many older men will go buy an attractive bright colored sports car, boat, watch, or even a sharp dressed clothing line. It's also important to note though as well they are many times the only ones who can afford to buy them!

It would appear though as seen before that the modern American has a desire to remain young looking and attractive, while exhibiting signs of maturity as well. Physical appearance is obviously important in how we are perceived and obviously has its benefits to prolonged life and health. In my personal observation when I go to the gym, there is always man or woman is trying to make their presence noted. This clothing (if some of it is labeled clothing) is normally extremely tight or showing off their alleged physical assets. I guess it is safe to say they are expressing themselves in ways that they want others to notice, no matter what they might say.

Martin Remland discusses another area I thought was noteworthy and I thought very interesting when it comes to how we perceive and look at each person. He says this:

---

[19] Ibid, 178.

"As applied to facial appearance, however the principle of youthfulness states that an attractive face contains some optimum blend of mature and immature features; it does not suggest that younger is necessarily better. If faces looked more attractive simply because they were younger looking, men and women with baby faces would look better than everyone else. While this is true of women's faces than it is of men's --- a nonthreatening appearance is more important than in men --- it overlooks the importance of adult facial features, which add a measure of strength and sexual competence to the appearance of the face."[20]

2. Physical Dimensions - Now in this area, let's break this into two sections where facial characteristics and the body's physical shape are discussed. Both are interesting of how they are perceived by each of us.

    a. *The Face* - Knapp and Hall in their book, *Nonverbal Communication in Human Interaction*, describe a study which was conducted by Langlois and Roggman in 1990 in which 96 college males and 96 females' pictures were taken. These photos were then collected and scanned by a video lens connected to a computer that converted each picture into a matrix of tiny digital units. The authors then allowed the computer to randomly select faces from the male and female photos. Additionally, the computer then generated composite photos of the selected persons and how the changes were viewed. As a result of this study they write;

    "Ratings by students showed that composite faces were more attractive than virtually any of the individual faces, and the most attractive faces were composites of 16 and 32 faces."[21]

---

[20] Remland, *Nonverbal Communication in Everyday Life*, 117.
[21] Knapp and Hall, *Nonverbal Communication in Human Interaction*, 182-183.

Why is this so? Read on. Furthermore in this study Knapp and Hall noted that Langlois and her colleagues acknowledged in some cases that people are perceived as attractive by large numbers of people even though their features obviously are not the population average. In fact, the most attractive faces are not likely to be average at all. The most attractive faces tend to emphasize those features associated with physically attractive faces. A woman, for example, would have a higher than average forehead, fuller than average lips, shorter than average jaw, and smaller than average chin or nose. They concluded their study by saying how we make perceptions within a few seconds and decide.

> "Because the face is so central in judgments of attractiveness, it is no surprise that is the source of stereotyping---often based in glances of a second or less."[22]

Because the physical attractiveness potential of one face to another, we must decide that we will treat each person fairly. This may sound simple in itself, but many times people may be inclined to show partiality to those who seem to be more attractive or appealing. Although this is not always fair to the other party when discriminatory, it is human nature to do so. This is why many times men take pictures with women who are physically very attractive, rather than an average woman who do not meet that exceptional level. I remember an old movie named, *Cannonball Run*, where two ladies drove a Lamborghini Diablo and tried to avoid tickets while speeding across the United States in a race. It didn't always work for them though either when they were later pulled over by a female police officer.

It is true that each one of us is more preferential to certain physical features in opposite sexes such as hair, eye colors, nose structure, jaw and cheek appearances we find more attractive.

In my former 200 hours of training in investigating adult and child sex crimes as a law enforcement officer, our training revealed that most child

---

[22] Ibid, 184.

sex offenders are preferential in these same characteristics when selecting a child victim. Although their preference is certainly much more sickening, the preferences are along the same lines we find preferential. In fact they show signs of preference in certain children's hair color, age, and physical structure. This is the next section we will be observing.

b. *The Body* - Knapp and Hall state there is an importance of understanding the physical body and how we treat people. In observations of body characteristics, we sometimes judge people by the way we view their physical appearance; even when it is not fair to the opposite party. Both state how we even decide what a person is like based upon our visual perception:

"Clearly the evidence shows we do associate certain personality and temperament traits with certain body builds. These expectations may or may not be accurate, but they do exist, and they are a part of the psychological mortar in interpersonal communication."[23]

The observation of *somatotypes* is mentioned by all the authors in this field as well. *Somatotypes* are perceptions of physical body sizes and dimensions which affect the perception of each person. All of the authors I've seen have identified in this book have similar views and comments in this area. These perceptions have definite consequences of how anyone might be observed without an interaction ever occurring.

Remland defines somatotypes as;

"Different types of human physiques of people that may be related to an individual's temperament or personality (Sheldon, 1940; Sheldon, Dupertuis, and McDermott, 1954)."[24]

i. Endomorphic- which is soft, round, and far, tends to be seen as lazy, weak, sympathetic agreeable, dependent, and good-natured.

---

[23] Ibid, 189.
[24] Remland, *Nonverbal Communication in Everyday Life*, 132.

ii. Ectomorphic- which is tall, thin, and fragile, is regarded as tense, nervous, suspicious, ambitious, quiet, and pessimistic.

iii. Mesomorphic- which is muscular and athletic is considered to be masculine, strong, good-looking, adventurous, and self-reliant. (Wells and Siegel, 1961)[25]

This might be why people based upon their human physiques observe each other and appear to have a natural connection. Many times this might occur if the other person is unknown to the other. For instance, if a person enters a restaurant and a person who is muscular is sitting inside; the other will normally greet the muscular person or will notice and acknowledge their presence. There seems to be a nonverbal connection to the common interest in that particular field. On the other hand, while it is not fair to do so, a muscular person might view a person in the same restaurant that is overweight as lazy and discount them. Although this view is incorrect and unfair to every individual who encounters it, the fact remains that in society this occurs every day.

3. Color - The color of the body has potential to become a great indicator as well in observing behaviors. Generally, a person who is of lighter skin tone may react more apparent when embarrassed by the changing of their skin tone to a flushed, indicating their embarrassment, whereas another of darker skin complexion may not appear as noticeable. But it doesn't end with just fair skin tones which are noticeable to people.
As history sadly indicates over the last two hundred years, the struggle with prejudice continues to this day and as a result causes problems in the interactional process as well. This is noted within the race of a person, which also is an effect of color. We would be wise to understand those who have been affected by these periods in history. It requires our sensitivity to people from varying backgrounds and possible struggles. We must learn to

---

[25] Ibid, 132.

treat people of any color with the respect and compassion of the Lord Jesus Christ. He did this with people from various backgrounds and national origins to share the Good News of the gospel. The Bible speaks this truth very clearly through the words of Peter;

> *"Then Peter opened his mouth, and said, of a truth I perceive that God is no respecter of persons: But in every nation he that feareth him, and worketh righteousness, is accepted with him"* (Acts 10:34-35, KJV).

Remland observes the same by saying;

> "Our race and ethnic identity is closely tied to our physical appearance (e. g., skin, color, facial features, and style of dress). Although racial classifications are regarded as scientifically invalid, the judgments we make about a person's race are part of everyday life."[26]

And it couldn't be any truer folks. In my past church experience in the early 1990's, I heard a statement from a person in the church say that a mixed race couple should have not been welcomed in the church. This was because because of their mixed marriage and interracial family. I remember telling the person that I (a young Christian at the time) lost a lot of respect for them on that day. I was met with a negative verbal response from that particular statement, but I really could have cared less. What a horrible thing to say to God's creation! God doesn't make junk. The pastor the following Sunday morning addressed the biblical view as stated by scripture to set the man's statement straight. Sadly, this attitude in America still remains to this day no matter where you are. I'm sure the skin tone on my face that day reflected my anger toward the man who spoke so cruel to that family.

---

[26] Ibid, 124.

4. Smell - Every person we encounter in the interactional process may even influence our response. Be careful. As you interact, you will come to perceive certain things about a person and possibly make a decision concerning the person by using smell. Knapp and Hall think Americans generally do not assign a meaning unless it is overpowering by saying:

> "Americans do not seem to rely consciously on their sense of smell for much interpersonal information, unless perspiration odor, breath, or some other smell is unusually strong or inappropriate to the situation."[27]

I do however believe the use of smell can also be used for great insight during occasions such as drug usage like marijuana which can be detected on the breath and clothing. Alcohol can also be discerned after a few seconds of interaction. We as pastors and leaders would be wise at these times to postpone any meeting and maybe reschedule the interaction. Normally this person will not normally remember the things discussed in the past anyway. We must further understand the person we are in contact with during these times is not in the right frame of mind to adequately come with all his faculties; especially when it comes to sharing the gospel. In addition, the ability to establish baseline behavior will be impossible due to the change in the person's temperament.

On the other hand, people allow prejudices simply because a person may have a body odor. Many times within our ministry at my church we have received a young man or woman within our congregation who exhibited an overpowering body odor. This could have created a barrier to communication for many people but our congregation was loving and receptive.

In one case in the past, we had a young man enter the church building one morning right before Sunday school. Because of his body odor, many would think at first smell to stay clear of him. We didn't know his story

---

[27] Knapp and Hall, *Nonverbal Communication in Human Interaction*, 195.

or his background though. After spending time with this young man, I found that he had been homeless for over a year and recently was able to find a place to stay near the church. It was a short walk for him to come to our church. Because of his previous year of living homeless, he had become so accustomed to not bathing that he no longer realized the body odor he was projecting to others around him. It was through many months of relationship building that I was able to speak to him about returning to societal norms of hygiene. He confided in me and said he was never aware of this until I spoke to him. He apologized for inconveniencing others around him. As a great testimony for the church, they from the onset lovingly welcomed him into the fellowship and he now serves the Lord Jesus Christ there. Oh, and by the way, he knew his bible better than many inside the fellowship! His Bible pages which were worn and dirty as well, but those many hours of washing his soul before the Lord in His Word made him perfectly clean.

5. Hair - Did you know that our hair affects the interactional process as well? Because most of our appearance on our face is governed or enhanced by the hair, it is wise to understand the implications of hair or lack thereof. It may even determine how the person seeks to be perceived. The care or lack of it though can also constitute some nonverbal indicators which should be observed as well.

Knapp and Hall observe some interesting information concerning men and hair. They share the differences between male and female hair and how they are perceived in society;

> "Most of the negative reactions against long hair are directed at males; negative reactions against hair that is too short or called "microbuzzes" are more likely to be directed at females. Some men are concerned about baldness as detracting from their own attractiveness,

but just as often, women report male baldness does not significantly detract from a male's attractiveness."[28]

That is comforting to some of us! But as society continues to change in the world we live within, change will be consistent in this area for sure. For instance, in today's society the scruffy beard on men is now acceptable because of the current culture in 2017. Although it may be offensive to some who were brought up in the 1950's when the clean-cut look was in, it might cause some unnecessary barriers to initial interaction. It must be understood that this in no way defines the person's personality, but many times they are sending signals. This is why initial responses must be shunned until a better understanding can be gained. This area will be covered in the following chapters where we look into the area of congruency.

6. Clothing - Clothing can tell you a lot about a person. Whether a person is neat or sloppy can tell a lot about the way a person thinks about them self or what they want to project. This can change as quickly as the clothes they wear. So be careful before you make a decision about what you think. Remland observes another area which is also important to you in determining nonverbal communication;

> "Most people have an image of the kind of person they want others to think they are. And whether that image happens to be hip, rebellious, conservative, young, affluent, healthy, or mature, we can use physical appearance to project the desired image. At the same time, we may also recognize the need to alter our appearance according to the situation."[29]

When we observe the way a person is dressed during the interactional process, we may be able to determine whether the person was in a hurry

[28] Ibid, 199.
[29] Remland, *Nonverbal Communication in Everyday Life*, 133.

which may appear sloppy, or wanted a positive reaction by dressing nicely. They might even project an image of their own suiting which might exude their character, personal perception, or projection. If we understand these we can gain insight into the person's interest and it may allow a smoother transition into a conversation which reaches the person by similar interests. If you can observe and implement these from the interim, you may have a better chance to initiate a more personal connection. It might also give us an idea of the value the person places upon physical things in their life.

Gestures and Posture

These are also physical signs which are given by the sender to anticipate understanding through interaction and acceptance. These you may be aware of and not even know it though. There are postures by the human body which signal behaviors which are consistent or relative to the situation. These gestures or postures can exhibit interest or lack of, comfort or uneasiness, nervousness or the need to create understanding by the other person in the process. To gain a simple understanding of each of these areas, I want to provide some helpful insight into these areas.

1. Gestures - Knapp and Hall suggest the importance of these functions and how they relate to verbal communication. They note the importance of how they relate to our daily conversations;

   "Gestures perform many functions. They may replace speech during dialogue, or when speech is not used at all. They may regulate the flow and rhythm of interaction, maintain attention, add emphasis or clarity to speech, help characterize and make memorable the content of speech, act as forecasters of forthcoming speech, and help speaker access and formulate speech."[30]

   EM Griffin gives a very simple definition of gestures. He states simply;

[30] Knapp and Hall, *Nonverbal Communication in Human Interaction*, 224.

"Gestures are any kind of body movement from the neck down."[31]

Even though this is partially true, I think that even the slightest head movement however can trigger a nonverbal cue as well. Especially if I roll my head around in a circle if a person is lecturing me or I nod that I understand what a person is saying to me. That nonverbal signal may communicate they really do or do not want to hear what is being said. Therefore, I would submit that the entire body sends cues and signals during this process. It's always nice to have someone nod their head once in a while to let you know they aren't asleep. I had a young man who wanted to meet with me in the past. As we began to talk, his head would start dropping slowly like he was going to sleep sitting up. I sometimes wonder if he was narcoleptic. As I would ask him if he heard me, he would reply "Gotcha." His head said no, with his voice saying yes. These meetings didn't last long unfortunately. He does periodically call me to talk. Maybe he was awake then.

Gestures can be used by hand signals which indicate known communication patterns to the recipient. As these signals are being sent, they characterize the content and direction of the speech which is being communicated to the other party. Some examples would be the index finger pointing in the direction of the object, a hand to the throat area to indicate choking, or palms opened facing upward. This might indicate that the person does not know the answer to the question being posed. Other types of gestures can determine more emphasis by the sender to accent or emphasize part of a conversation. At times these gestures can be repetitive to the point they no longer produce emphasis and become distracting or no longer relied upon for meaning. When they reach this point these gestures become distractive or abusive in nature and serve no further influence in the interaction process. Then you end up tuning them out. Think of the last time you might have received that abusive "middle

---

[31] E. M. Griffin, *Making Friends and Making Them Count* (Downer Grove, IL: Inter Varsity Press, 1987), 118.

finger" from someone who was angry at an innocent mistake while you were driving in traffic. Hopefully, you weren't interested in communicating anything further to them. It might ruin your testimony from that point. Discount that gesture.

2. Posture - Posture is another important area you need to become familiar. While some postures are simple to understand, others can determine the level of interest or disinterest by the person whom you will interact. Leaning forward might indicate interest by the listener, while the same leaning forward posture can be a signal of aggressive behavior. Each of these postures will have additional indicators which might signal change in behavior. Leaning back in a chair may indicate the person's interest listening. This might be that they feel comfortable enough to relax in the environment they are in. On the other hand, the other leaning back in a chair might signal disconnection with the other party. Everyone has seen someone roll back their chair when something comes they don't want to hear. It could be a disconnection or something even more dangerous.

Knapp and Hall indicate some other interesting observations concerning what they call "interactional synchrony." He gives a few terms which will help you understand the level of identification with people:

    a. *Matching* - Without always being very aware of it, human beings commonly tend to mimic the mannerisms, facial expressions, postures, and other behaviors of the people they interact with. This has been called the "chameleon effect --not because people, like chameleons, change colors to match their environment, but because people change their postures, gestures, and mannerisms to match those of their interaction partners.[32]

    b. *Meshing* - Another way of examining the phenomenon of interaction synchrony has been to observe the ongoing co-occurrence of changes in movement and speech by each of two interactants... like matching behavior, meshing has also linked

---

[32] Knapp and Hall, *Nonverbal Communication in Human Interaction*, 245.

to conversational satisfaction and liking for one's interaction partner.[33]

These interactions can be seen in their head movements, facial expressions which affirm their behavior with the other parts of their body (congruence). They also give some good insight to the potential connection between the two parties in the interaction. It's interesting to see this in action and how valid Knapp' and Hall's point are so true.

The Florida Department of Law Enforcement teaches a similar technique in what is called *mirroring* in the interview process. This is taught to special agents who spend a lot of time interviewing complex and demanding cases. In order for them to have a good connection with the victim / suspect, they have to put the person at ease. This effect of *mirroring* is to determine the level of connection with the person in the meeting. In this *mirror effect* the following suggestions are made:

1. Match the posture of the individual.
2. Watch the blink rate of the eye.
3. Listen for voice intonations (patterns or pitch changes within the voice).
4. Look for breathing rates.
5. Listen for vocabulary changes.[34]

Then the recommendation is to the following "Mirror Test" to determine the level of connection to the meeting;

> "Mirror the person for a short time, then change your position and see if they respond"[35]

This test is used to determine if the connection has been made between the two parties involved and determines the feedback when it occurs. If it has; mirroring has occurred.

---

[33] Ibid, 249.
[34] Florida Department of Law Enforcement, *Investigative Interviews Advanced Course #047*, Tallahassee, FL: Criminal Justice Standards and Training Commission, 1989.
[35] Ibid, 7.

I have used this technique many times in the past in interviews in the law enforcement and public realm and can tell you with certainty that it works. In order to test this in your own life, recognize that there also needs to be a high level of trust within the relationship and whom you *mirror* the behavior. I have myself intentionally crossed my arms in a conversation and found that within a few seconds or so that the person begins to cross their arms as well. This is not a sign of them blocking me out, but a sign of *mirroring*. This is always a good sign that you have connected with the person so don't laugh when it happens; otherwise you might have to explain your action to them.

The Effect of Touch

Touch can be used for many communicative purposes to include but not limited to encouragement, positive reinforcement, influence, healing, and symbolism. Touch can also have negative and positive effects when used, but can also become a powerful tool when applied correctly by you. The areas of body contact can also tell you a lot about the level of comfort or offense one can send to another by personal touches on the body. Touches on the top of the shoulder may convey encouragement, while touching the shoulder to the upper back may make the person feel quite uncomfortable. This depends on the limitations or unfamiliarity level of that relationship. The rule here is the better the relationship, the less chance of offense.

Touch is used as reinforcement in different types of interactions where verbal communication is not required and sometimes is one of the most effective. Henry Calero states in his book, *The Power of Nonverbal Communication,* the importance of touch and dangers which could be expressed without knowing it had occurred:

> "So, some argue, the safe play is to avoid touching
> people altogether. Better to avoid the matter entirely
> than do it badly and come off like a neurotic or a creep.
> But that attitude misses a critical element of nonverbal

communication. It also breeds a sterile approach to dealing with people that, frankly, isn't effective."[36]

In other cases of touch he also says how important is in infantile relationship:

> "The power of touch is so effective that studies conducted at the Minnesota-based Mayo Clinic have demonstrated premature babies grow 40 percent faster than those who do not receive the same amount of stroking. Other studies also reveal early tactile experience is crucial toward later mental and emotional development in humans."[37]

The basic rules of touch can also be bypassed by you in times of extreme duress by people involved in situations such as death, hospitalization, severe illnesses, etc. It is at these times when people need the experience of touch. It is also at these times touch of another human being conveys care without words ever being spoken. We all know this. Some of these acts are regarded as off limits during normal interaction, but calming and reinforcing in times like this. Calero sums this whole section by stating what a smart person should do;

> "A smart person who understands nonverbal communication can recognize the signs that someone is willing to lower ordinary inhibitions about physical contact. These signs can include open or upturned palms, a slow head tilt, and a slight shrug of the shoulders, a raised eyebrow and eye contact with a smile. But, even if you see the signs, keep the contact light and quick."[38]

In some instances, as any of you know when the visit to a hospitalized

---

[36] Calero, *The Power of Nonverbal Communication*, 13.
[37] Ibid, 13.
[38] Ibid, 13.

person and prayer begins you will notice the person's hand is extended. This is to receive the pastor or other person's hand in the linking of their hands for that purpose. On the other hand (metaphorically), the hospitalized person may extend their hand at the onset of the meeting. These are clear situations where you have been given permission to bypass the normal rules because the person has reached out to you (no pun intended).

In another situation where a critical event has transpired, you have to realize that the effect of touch may be the simple hand on the top of the shoulder to convey compassion without ever stating a word. I have used this effect numerous times within ministry and law enforcement purposes to convey that someone is there with them during their time of need. It also allows a personal connection while in the midst of silent prayer for the person. Some of those touches may leave lasting impressions in the person's life.

Whatever effect of touch you use, you must be familiar with what may be perceived by the recipient. In these cases, the depth of the relationship has a determinative factor in these effects. For instance, a hug to a total stranger might be completely off limits due to becoming creepy or inappropriate during a casual meeting, but the loss of a child by a parent might warrant that extending of love and compassion.

The Expressions of the Face

Emotion can be seen through various signs of the face such as eyebrow movement, smiles which also convey different meanings, and skin tone color. The face is where most of the emotions of a person can be observed. It is also the number one area of feedback during the interactional process. There are so many identifiers located within the facial area though. It also happens to be our physical focal point while in conversations during the majority of our conversations unless there is an unwanted distraction that contends for our attention. Intentional or non-intentional facial feedback can be observed by both you and the other person during this process without the other even knowing what happened. Burgoon, Guerrero and Floyd state how our culture is also very good at interpreting expressions;

"Most researchers agree that facial expressions of happiness and to a lesser extent of sadness, anger, fear, surprise, and disgust, are universally understood... although some researchers suggest that the accuracy of decoding these motions is highest for Western cultures"[39] Furthermore they assert, "The universality of emotional expression may also be limited to these primary emotions."[40]

With this said, the pastor has a better chance of understanding his people within a setting inside the United States and with their people. This also limits the scope of the study in this book as well. To understand some of these behaviors, I want you to understand that other identifiers in the face will also be present instead of just looking for one indicator. So therefore you will see a number of indicators at one time during an interaction. Knapp and Hall identify these as what they calls "affect blends." They state no matter how complicated it may appear, in reality it's not that hard to decipher;

"People do not always portray pure or single emotional states, in which all the parts of the face show a single emotion. Instead, the face conveys multiple emotions. These are called affect blends and may appear on the face in numerous ways. For example, one emotion is suggested by one facial area, and another is suggested by another area, as when brows are raised in surprise and lips are pressed in anger. Or two different emotions are shown in one part of the face, as when one brow is raised as in surprise, and the other is lowered as in anger."[41]

It is important for you to culminate the amount of emotions you see

---

[39] Burgoon, Guerrero, and Floyd, *Nonverbal Communication*, 44.
[40] Ibid, 44.
[41] Knapp and Hall, *Nonverbal Communication in Human Interaction*, 301.

and determine what is happening within the person. Simply taking one facial expression for its meaning may not be the intention of the sender. If you take one expression and try to determine what is going on inside the person you risk losing connection with the person. You may also misunderstand the intent of their interaction. With the numerous areas to consider at one time, some of these individual areas can be observed by actions such as:

1. Yawning and stretching to convey sleepiness or lack of sleep or boredom.
2. A consistent slow closing of the eyelids to convey boredom or sleepiness.
3. Rolling the eyes and looking toward another direction to convey lack of interest.
4. Winking could illustrate a close relational reinforcement to a flirtatious interest to a person to whom no relationship exists. You will be better off not using this indicator since this could be misunderstood at times. Because of the potential for the way it might be received it is better off not used and sometimes can be received as creepy.
5. A puffing up of the cheeks to convey a condition of overeating or being full.
6. Drawing the lips to one side to convey the thoughts of another in response to a question. This may allow the person who posed the question to allow time for a response.
7. A wide opening of the mouth, eyelids or lifting of the eyebrows to convey surprise.
8. Eyebrows which lower in the inner face area to express discouragement or sadness.
9. A change in the color of the skin which might indicate embarrassment or potential anger (turning flush after a receiving a response).
10. Closing of the eyelids tightly to convey expressions or relation to painful experiences.

As I stated before, many of these indicators could be used together to convey complex expressions which may be non-volitional by the sender. By watching each of these in harmony together a person can gauge the level of readability and transparency from people. Then you will be able to determine if the response is genuine. A lot to take in right? Well, that's not all. Hang in there, you are doing well!

The Effects of the Eye

Gazing, dilation and constriction, and rapid movement effect could also have meaning during your interactions. These areas of feedback seldom are observed by the person you are interacting. This type of nonverbal communication is not easily observed or controlled in deceptive or stimulated situations either. So these types can be good indicators since the person seldom knows they are being transmitted. Although nervousness can be attributed in these effects they need to be discerned in conjunction with other cues in the interactional process. Henry Calero tells us how the eye may respond in a couple of situations that the person never intends or knows is happening:

> "For example, its common knowledge that, when a person sees something that is attractive or pleasing, his pupils will dilate. Elsewhere, I've mentioned the drug belladonna, which causes the pupils to dilate, means beautiful woman in Italian. A poker player's eyes will do the same thing when he sees a pair of aces as the hole cards in a game of Texas Hold'em."[42]

As a result, many poker players wear glasses to keep from being observed by eye related changes which signal his hand in the game. These can be observed on most television programs which are on the air at this time. These acts are not to be "cool," but to keep other players from discerning the hand of the player by his eyes. On the other hand it is interesting to

---

[42] Calero, *The Power of Nonverbal Communication*, 69.

note the implications of interest which might could exhibited by a person who shows signs of intimate interest in another. Young men might learn a lot here and avoid uncomfortable mistakes.

Another area to consider is the abuse or overuse of abuse of prescription and illegal drugs (Oxycodone and other forms of pain medicines, "Crack" and powder cocaine, Crystal Meth, Heroine, etc.) can alter the way the eye reacts. For instance, a person who is using large amounts of pain drugs over a period of time may experience overly watery eyes and redness. The pupils may be dilated as well. On the other hand, you should take the time to see if it is an allergy condition which has caused their eyes to water and redden because of seasonal conditions or exposure to allergies. In either circumstance, you would be wise to take all the nonverbal indicators and put them together to determine if there is enough supportive information to make a clear discernment. Most of the time it doesn't take much, as most people will tell you they are miserable with a bad case of allergies. Few times are people going to express that they are abusing drugs in your presence.

Calero notes something interesting as well which law enforcement use at times. He says:

> "Police inspectors and interrogators also ask a lot of questions to those who are under investigation. And they always look for a change in the blink rate that might signify areas where the person is trying to cover something or might be lying. And psychiatrists are also aware of the significance of the blink rate when they attempt to get personal disclosure from a patient who is trying desperately to conceal it from them."[43]

Although I have never taken the time to observe blink rates of potential suspect(s) during my career, I think anyone inside a police station is likely to be on guard during an interview. How would you act? On the other

[43] Ibid, 70.

I Understand What You Are Not Saying

hand, Calero states these facial expressions can be self-induced to provide convincing results if enough energy is placed into it. I would agree with him along with other efforts that the person uses to appear genuine or honest.

> "A person is capable of altering his facial expression if he puts all his mental energy into it. This is exactly as the great acting teacher, Stanislavski predicted, 'You should think about the emotion as hard as you can, the result will produce itself.'"[44]

This is why the need to become observant in the process of observing nonverbal communication through *all the senses* is so important. This allows us to have the ability to determine the full extent of the behavior from the individual. These behaviors may signal other things in determining the real reason for the behavior and allow you to help the person. By understanding what these indicators are and how they conflict when sent is imperative. It may also help to determine when the person is being superficial or telling a lie. Walters explains regarding truth and deception;

> "No single kinesic behavior, verbal or nonverbal by itself is proof of truth of deception."[45]

Because of this statement, one indicator is never all inclusive to the perceived behavior. This is the reason we develop a relationship from the beginning, so that departures from norms will be noticed. This is where we begin to start with your initial contact and build the relationship. From this point you will begin to see normal patterns of behavior. It's called *baseline behavior.*

---

[44] Ibid, 71.
[45] Stan B. Walters, *Practical Kinesic Interview and Interrogation* (Indianapolis, IN: Stan Walter and Associates, 2009), 8.

Baseline Indicators

This area is probably one of the most important sections of this book because it culminates all you have read in the previous chapters. This area will help you to understand what the person is like under normal circumstances and environment. The nonverbal indicators we have learned about so far will allow us to know what they are. Then we begin to observe the comfort level and behavior of the person. In short, this is what the person looks like in their daily nonverbal life. These can be observed as you meet in a setting where they can feel free to be themselves. This is why I stated earlier the importance the development of the environment. Their behavior will reflect the way they act in a normal setting without outside influences. This is what they look like at home by themselves. When we have a good understanding of the real person under their normal circumstances, we can begin to interact in a way that will produce success, harmony, and express our compassion for others. Remember, everyone has a front they want you to see, but there is a different person inside and only the Holy Spirit knows them best.

Navarro states how he used to observe and interact concerning these baseline conditions when interviewing suspects of crimes while with the FBI:

> "When I interviewed criminal suspects at the FBI, the last thing I wanted was to intimidate them or put them on the defensive. One the contrary: I wanted to put them at ease; make sure they had something to drink; see to their comfort. And while they got comfortable, I observed their every move, from their posture as they approached me to their eye blink rate as we sat together. Why? Because in order to know how an individual exhibits discomfort, you must first observe how they behave when comfortable. Once you establish a person's comfort behaviors as a baseline, you'll watch for departures from the baseline as signs of discomfort. For example, it's often assumed

that crossed arms signal defensiveness. Not so, if a person characteristically stands this way. I have a friend who often crosses his arms pensively during conversation. It's when he abruptly changes his position that I attune to possible discomfort."[46]

Any changes in previous behavior by the person should be observed which would depart from the normal nonverbal behavior at this time. Remember, this requires *time spent* with the person to establish baseline conditions. These are more easily recognized *over time and experience* with the person. When changes in behavior change significantly, you must remember the time it occurred and what was mentioned. Then note the changes in nonverbal indicators, and how they are being exhibited to you.

From this point, you must watch all the indicators which signal trouble within the person, so you can later use these to assist in how to help the person. These changes should be observed in proper context within the situation you are meeting. It is significantly important to establish a normal behavior in the interim before further progress can be made. Without proper baseline behavior established from the start, the interaction and its effect cannot be established correctly. This could very well lead to an improper reading of the person's behavior.

As a result these definitions and effects provide a relative understanding for anyone who wants to interact with people. It will also raise the level of your awareness in the interactional process. As each of these indicators are noted and integrated, you can become more skillful in the interactional process. In addition, we will begin to know the *whole* person we are meeting. This baseline will provide us with a wealth of knowledge in the interactions to come. Then, the information from our previous encounters will help us establish normal behavior for the person.

Neff also notes the importance of understanding the role you play in the nonverbal communication process;

---

[46] Joe Navarro, *Louder Than Words* (New York, NY: Harper Collins Publishers, 2009), 36.

"Words do have power, but observers conclude that the nonverbal message system may have an even greater power. Some social scientists have argued that 93 percent of the emotional impact of a message comes from nonverbal sources. Others have reasoned more convincingly that the figure is closer to 65 percent (Adler and Towne, 2003, p.223). Regardless of the precise figure, it is clear that a large part of the emotional impact of a message is borne through nonverbal communication (Burgoon, 1994). The effective pastor will need to have a clear understanding of the role of the nonverbal message system."[47]

Whatever you might think throughout this section, learning to read nonverbal behavior doesn't come easily. It takes plenty of time and attention on the front end of the interactional process. It will lend itself many years of successful connections in the future if you continue. Remember though, the goal is to interact, connect, and help the person you are interacting with, not to get a leg up on them and prove you can manipulate them. God forgive us if we do.

---

[47] Neff, *A Pastors Guide to Interpersonal Communication*, 77.

CHAPTER FOUR

My Methodology for Pastoral Nonverbal Communication

When I began my research in late 2011 for my doctoral thesis in this topic, I sought to understand what pastors thought about the nonverbal communication process. This was a field I really felt led to understand and to share what I learned with pastors all over America in this particular field of study.

In order to get a proper understanding of what interest or knowledge was known in this particular field of study, I electronically polled church's pastors of the Florida Baptist Convention, within the St. Johns River Baptist Association. This Association is located within the counties of St. Johns, Flagler and Putnam counties, within the State of Florida. These are located in Northeast Florida. These 50 plus churches comprise the locale in which I also served as a pastor in the Northeast Florida area. The association has an Executive Director who assists struggling churches, starting new churches, outreach events, mission trips, and other projects, etc. Each church is autonomous to itself. This region has churches with memberships of less than 50 members ranging to over 1500 in attendance each week. So there is a great diversity amongst the three county areas of membership as well as pastoral experience. This I thought would provide a good base of diversity amongst the field I was polling.

The level of education for each pastor within this association was as varied as the membership within this three county region. Some pastors had Bible degrees from two year colleges, while others held terminal degrees from varying institutions. Some were reasonably new pastors, while others were well tenured in their service to the Lord with specialties in various fields of their own course studies.

To determine an understanding and potential interest by each pastor for this topic, I sent an electronic questionnaire to each pastor through the Associational Office requesting feedback. These electronic questionnaires were then forwarded through the secretary of the Director of Missions for this association to each pastor's individual email account. My request to the pastors was to complete each survey and send the responses back to my personal email account for review and analysis. Each pastor was given a period of three weeks to complete the survey and email their responses for collection. This was so I could determine my findings prepare, collate, and analyze the results. I never understood how significant this undertaking would become and the varied responses I would receive back from those pastors.

After sending the preliminary questionnaire to the secretary of the association, she responded to me. She told me only roughly 35 pastors had email accounts and was in the process of updating their personal profiles to insure accurate home and email addresses. She stated she would need more time than I could ask for the responses since many pastors did not regularly respond to her requests at any given time. So this lowered the amount which could be surveyed from 58 to now 35 pastors. That became roughly 60% of the Association. To try to send the other questions to pastor's home address via U. S. Mail, I knew would take too long for the response needed for my thesis project.

Of the 35 churches electronically surveyed, I asked each pastor a selection of questions concerning the nonverbal communication process and how it could be used within a ministry setting. Each of these questions was posed to determine an *initial* level of understanding of this topic within their own ministries. In addition, each question was meant to build upon the previous to determine the level of understanding of the pastors for the topic. Some questions had two or three additional questions within the numbered to determine their level of understanding or application within their ministries.

Before pastors began responding to the questions, I asked each pastor who would respond to take the time and prayerfully consider the assessment. This meant taking the time they needed, praying, and asking God to show them in sincerity how they should reply to the questions. I also asked pastors to determine where they might fall short and to respond with an openness which would not be viewed as weakness, but meekness, and teachability. This way I could receive honest results and it would increase the chance of my research to give you a fair representation of the data (as well as my thesis mentors).

So, here is the list of the following questions which were posed to pastors and a second group of follow-up questions which were sent after (of the 35 listed above):

First Questionnaire:

1. Do you know what the nonverbal communication process is? If you do not know, would you be interested in learning further?

    The purpose of this question was to determine if some pastors understood the process since the level of education of pastors within the association was so varied. I couldn't take the risk of them not understanding the topic since many pastors were adults with limited seminary or college education and/or training in the field of nonverbal communication. I also realize many seminaries have a full load of classes which cover a wide range of areas of ministry and did not cover a lot of communication topics. This would be true especially with this topic. The second question also allowed me to determine in the interim if these polled pastors might be interested in the results of my findings after completion. My goal was to stimulate some interest, and then possibly leave a few takeaways with each person for the future. I wanted to determine the reality of interest in the field for further research questions in this field.

2. Do you know how to recognize nonverbal indicators of people when you interact with them daily?

    I assumed in the beginning of the survey that most pastors

interact with people on a daily basis. Let's at least hope this happens each day. If it doesn't, how can we become their pastor? I posed this question to determine whether pastors, although interacting with people knew if there was something more to the communication process than simply speaking to each other by verbal communication. It also allowed the pastors to give me a few examples which might help me to understand their view of what nonverbal communication really is when they see it. I also wanted to see if there were going to be some stories which came from them which would allow me to see the reality of Question #1 being fleshed out in their understanding of the topic.

3. Could you readily recognize nonverbal indicators in an interaction? If so, could you determine what might be said before the verbal communication began?

This question was built upon the previous question with the possibility of potential understanding of some pastors and whether they could identify nonverbal indicators within interaction. This question also performed the task of digging deeper into the knowledge base of each pastor who might have a basic understanding of the process by determining their level of comprehension of indicators or emotional intelligence of the individual they are interacting.

4. Would you be interested in learning further about the nonverbal communication process if you do not feel completely comfortable with any of the answers above?

To cover all the above questions, I wanted to give pastors who were surveyed an "out" for some that might have no understanding of the process but wanted to provide limited responses to the author in an attempt to help him with his project. This "out" was to allow pastors a way to save face without telling me about their lack understanding without feeling embarrassed. The purpose of the questionnaires was not to make pastors feel embarrassed because of their lack of understanding but only to gain a fair assessment of the information collected to insure an accurate analysis of the information received.

Second Questionnaire:

To probe the matter further, I asked the same pastors a second series of questions several weeks later to obtain further information for this topic. The second list of questions was sent again through the St. Johns River Baptist Association secretary who forwarded them again to all pastors in the Association via the same communication outlet as before.

1. Do you understand the qualifications of the pastor as presented in 1 Timothy 3:1-7? Second, since communication with your people is a spiritual encounter, do you know what scripture requires of the pastor in this interaction? Third, if you understand this, what would affect the process of the spiritual interaction?

   To survey pastors further and discover their need to understand the biblical requirement of them in the nonverbal communication process, I hoped would be pretty easy to define. I was surprised by some of the later responses to this question as well. I also wanted to determine if pastors understood the process as a spiritual encounter, because many times we don't even think about that realm in daily interaction. Third, I wanted to ask pastors if they understood why scripture was not only important to their calling, but should be a natural part of their lifestyle when interacting with people. Fourth, I knew some pastors would understand their calling as well as their requirement to be all scripture commands; however I wanted to see what their ideas were that might affect the process. This question allowed the most experienced pastor to respond to the question and allowed the most inexperienced to give input as well.

2. Do you use these biblical mandates within the interactional process to further the communication process from scripture such as, establishing trust, reliability, confidentiality, etc.? If "yes" to this

particular question, how did you do so? If not, what is preventing you from doing so in the future? What is preventing you from doing so right now?

To probe the matter further regarding the understanding of scriptural interaction, I wanted to determine how they began to interact with people and what identifiers might be important to them before, during, and after the interactional process. If they used certain methods, I wanted to probe pastors further by possibly determining what was being used and what levels of success were they obtaining. In closing, if they were not using these methods or others, why were they not trying to do so? The last question posed a challenge to them to think about their interaction in the future. As with the Word of God, when a spiritual encounter occurs and when instruction is given, it demands a response by the individual.

3. Do you understand the two natures which still exist within a redeemed person and how the natures affect the interactional process? Do you see this as an influence to interaction?

While interacting, I too understand the battle of our natures which war against the soul in a daily environment. In this, my question was posed to determine if pastors understood how these daily battles may signal a carnal lifestyle which is overtaking the spiritual. If pastors could understand how these natures affect the interactional process and battle for their soul, what kind of influence might they have on the person in the interaction? If there was an influence to the interaction, was it positive or negative in nature and why? Again, my question was given to stimulate an articulation of the interactional process in a life experience which could be explained by pastors through a personal experience.

4. Do you have any idea of what you might learn about the process or if could you observe the two natures of man in communication and which one is more prevalent? What might you expect in return if you understood the process?

In the last question, I wanted to give pastors something to think about when interacting with people who are being controlled by something other than the Spirit of God in the interactional process. I used this question to probe the level of understanding of the requirements for the pastor as mentioned in 1 Timothy 3 and how to balance them with the person's responses in the interaction. Last, my question asked them look into their self and find a greater understanding of the process. I wanted to get each pastor to think about how much more effective they might be as a result of learning more.

I closed each email with a special thanks to all who took the time to respond to my interest and study in this topic. I really understand how busy and hectic a day can get very quick and early in each pastor's day. I also understand all the pulls each of us have each day and wanted them to know I shared their same burden. I also asked pastors who wanted further information regarding the findings of my research to contact me later after all the collection, assessment, and conclusions were complete. This concluded the assessment process.

Are you mildly interested in what they had to say? Turn to the next chapter and you will see what I learned. It might even shock you at times when you read some of the findings; although if you have been in ministry long enough you might already have an idea of what lies ahead.

CHAPTER FIVE

The Findings of Surveys Collected from Pastors

Over the next few weeks, emailed surveys began to flow back into my respective email account with each one's feedback. I started to collect the responses and began collating the information for each question for evaluation. Some I received were sent by U. S. Mail to the Associational Office. I collected those remaining during my next trip to the office.

Out of the first 35 questionnaires sent to pastor's emails, only 19 pastors responded to the questionnaires. Were you surprised? These responses comprise about 64% of the questionnaires sent to pastors for their input after a reduction once again from the initial effort to reach all 50 plus pastors in the Association. Most answers from them were very short (and maybe because they were too busy) while a few were somewhat longer, depending on the level of interaction in the particular question. Some pastors also interacted by email outside of the questionnaire by explaining some of their concerns about the nonverbal communication process. Some shared stories about how they felt the nonverbal communication process had affected their ministry; even until today. As a result, I recorded the following feedback for the first questionnaire sent. So here's what I observed from the data:

First Questionnaire:

1st Question- Do you know what the nonverbal communication process is? If you do not know, would you be interested in learning further?

Approximately 95% of the pastors surveyed stated they understood the topic; however only in the basic or overt sense. They knew about it, what it was, but only enough to sometimes get themselves in trouble by trying to apply their own methods in nonverbal communication.

Five of them responded saying they could not believe this topic had never been researched from within a church ministry setting, especially after the increase of violence against pastors and churches in America today. Their concern stemmed from my indication of interest in this field of study for understanding and how it might help improve interaction. Their concerns of violence were warranted as well with the world we live within today.

Most responded by expressing their interest in greater understanding of subtle indicators. But what is subtle and what is not subtle enough to notice? I guess that depends upon the perception level of each individual person. Most however, indicated they knew the indicators were varied from person to person because of the general makeup of each person but wanted to know how to gain a better understanding.

The remaining 5% thought they had a good enough understanding and thought they needed no further assistance. Of this 5% who responded with confidence, they indicated they felt reasonably comfortable with the process and were not interested in learning further. Lastly, one pastor of this 5% stated he was not interested since he didn't have time to do anything more than he was doing on a day to day basis. While I understand his frustration with being super busy each day, it stills leaves a blind spot in his ministry. It might even save someone or even your own life one day. We can't do it all folks and that is why God has given us the Body of Christ to serve. For the one pastor who responded that he had no further time to do anything I would say this; we must learn to allow the body of Christ to function with each part doing theirs. We need to learn to delegate and allow God to produce the results through His body. And besides, we can't do it all. God never intended it that way anyway. 1 Corinthians 12:12-27 tells us how important we each are to the body of Christ.

2nd Question- Do you know how to recognize nonverbal indicators of people when you interact with them daily?

100% indicated they understood what the process was from daily interaction with people but had never been given insight to how the process works within an instructional setting. 5 percent of these questioned felt fairly confident in the process. This 5 percent who were fairly confident were men who had education backgrounds in the field of communication or had expansive college or seminary degree. I gained a lot this insight from my relationship with these men or through the Associational Executive Director who knows each pastor personally. Five percent from the first surveyed question stated they understood it in its infancy and had other things which were capturing their attention at present. The remaining 95 percent for the second question stated they had encounters with people in which they were not sure how to respond because of the nonverbal indicators. Each of them further said they thought they understood some of the indicators, but were interested in obtaining further information on areas they might not be familiar.

Interestingly enough, of these 95 percent of responses, about 70 percent of pastors indicated they felt anything they could learn more about the process would help them in counseling or interaction with their people on a daily basis. These men stated they understood the process but weren't sure how the indicators might affect the rest of the interaction. I hope you fall into this 70 percentile of pastors who want to learn more about the process. Your reading of this book tells me there is a pretty good chance that you fall into this category. I am proud that you are willing to take some time to learn how you can become a better communicator with your people. It will pay off in the long run if you take the time to learn to use the process effectively and God will bless your efforts as you do.

3rd Question- Could you readily recognize nonverbal indicators in an interaction? If so, could you determine what might be said before the verbal communication began?

About roughly 80 percent indicated they would feel better prepared to respond correctly to the needs of their people if they knew what situation they might encounter prior to engaging in the verbal process, especially if their safety was a concern.

Most men surveyed indicated they were not sure how to determine the differences from each interaction or how to determine the cues which might be given when their people met with them. 35 percent indicated they would also like to know if their lives could be endangered by being able to notice the potential danger indicators which could be exhibited by a person before violence occurred. Within this percentage, each indicated they felt very uneasy around some of their people at times. These responses indicated interest on how to identify key indicators which could signal danger. Some mentioned their nervousness at times when dealing with people who may have been a danger to themselves as well as the pastor. Each expressed interest in potential suicide/domestic violence or even homicidal acts and how to negotiate through the process of identifying these types of behaviors.

One gentleman answered his question with a story of how he called the police in one case when the person exhibited what he felt were suicidal tendencies, which were later a cry for attention to his spouse but exhibited improperly. This story he shared revealed his embarrassment, communication shortcomings, and misunderstanding he had as a result of the incident. He said he did not understand the behavior of his parishioner at the time and decided to act just in case something terrible occurred. He later lost the family to another church because of the lack of connection, violation of trust, and hurt feelings from the family. He stated his response failed the family by having an opportunity to be an effective minister in their time of need. He told me he wanted to help the family, but didn't understand what was happening at the time inside the man. It though, was too late because of the damage which had occurred. This story is one of many I have heard from pastors and other church leaders during this research and to this date. A lot of them acted in what they perceived to be in the best interests of their people only to misunderstand the signals.

4th Question- Would you be interested in learning further about the nonverbal communication process if you do not feel completely comfortable with any of the answers above?

95 percent of responses in this question indicated they would be interested on how to better themselves in the nonverbal communication process. This is a huge number. They felt this would help them to understand what was on a person's mind before hearing the spoken word. All said they understood the process would not be easy, but needed some sort of way to determine if they could establish indicators which would signal changes of behavior in their people. Then it would allow them to effectively connect with their people in time of crisis. Some even indicated an interest in a way to understand the process without having to take a collegiate level course in nonverbal communication. In fact a great number of men stated they did not have time within their current ministry to take more classes and might benefit from my research. This made me feel quite a bit better that the research I was conducting would be of benefit and not something that no one had an interest or felt was superficial. My goal was to help, not hinder pastors in the future. This is why I created a "hands-on" book that can be used as reference for future encounters.

Second Questionnaire:

Of the 35 pastors' questionnaires emailed for the second set of questions, 11 pastors responded to me with their responses. These responses were from roughly the same pastors who responded to the first emailed questionnaires, although obviously fewer in numbers this time. Some became vaguer in the answers in this questionnaire. Only one called me for clarification of one of the questions to make sure he understood the question properly before responding. Because of the vagueness from many, it allowed me to see the lack of depth in the understanding in this field previously mentioned. When answers got shorter or unanswered, it signaled many didn't have the level of understanding to respond to the questions or either didn't have time to respond in detail. I believe for most; it was for the first reason.

1st Question – Do you understand the qualifications of the pastor as presented in 1 Timothy 3:1-7? Since communication with your people is a spiritual encounter, do you know what scripture requires of the pastor in this interaction? If you understand this, what would affect the process of the spiritual interaction?

Approximately 90 percent responded they knew the qualifications of a pastor were important and biblical. This was comforting for the 90 percent; but scary that the other 10 percent did not really state it clearly. The 90 percent responded they knew the qualifiers affected their character and communication process with a person. All of them said they knew they were the spiritual example and leader for the flock. They also said how it made them careful in how they communicated with their people because of their calling and how they might be viewed. One man responded by stating he understood the process well enough however did not fully understand how the scripture (1 Timothy 3) would interact in the nonverbal communication process. A legitimate question right? The last question remained fairly vague with their responses, with mostly this one being left unanswered.

2nd Question – Do you use these biblical mandates within the interactional process to further the communication process from scripture such as, establishing trust, reliability, confidentiality, etc.? If "yes" to this particular question, how did you do so? If not, what is preventing you from doing so in the future? What is preventing you from doing so right now?

Nearly the same response (about 90 percent) was also in this question as well. Most pastors responded by stating "yes" that they used the biblical mandates within the interactional process. Pastors who replied "yes" said if the people whom the pastor ministers to has doubts about his character, they would be less likely to trust the communication in the future.

Additionally, more responded they were keenly aware of the importance of being men of character and integrity. By this statement, they felt it was more important to be what God wanted them to be, rather than what was accomplished in the interactional process. When the answer was "no" (10 percent) pastors responded in two areas. One area determined to have been based on the pastor's level of ministry experience. This was due to some being in the pastorate for less than five years. The second man answered who never understood the process because of his lack of training in communication. The more experienced pastors who were surveyed responded that their understanding of the interactional experience took a lot of time over the years in full-time ministry. These pastors said they understood the importance of trust and creditability to their people, but only knew it only occurred over time. One responded with his being, "graciously forthright" with his people even when at times it might be hurtfully received. He said he made mistakes in his past to spare a person's feelings and said one thing to one person and another thing to another person to appease them. He later learned his desire to keep people happy only resulted in distrust. This man leads a large church within the region. One other man responded he felt the need to be honest with people at all costs. He felt his honesty with a person no matter what was more important than worrying about how it might be received in the future. He saw this as a measure of personal integrity. This pastor as well currently leads another larger church within the association. It is obvious these pastors took their personal integrity very seriously and I compliment them in their quest to do so. We need more men of integrity who serve God like these in our pulpits today.

3rd Question – Do you understand the two natures which still exist within a redeemed person and how the natures affect the interactional process? Do you see this as an influence to interaction?

Most men (90 percent) experienced in ministry responded that they saw the nature of man was an obvious area for them to consider in the communication process. They responded by saying they were currently using this knowledge as a guide to determine the level of honesty, integrity and transparency from the person during the interaction. Remaining men (10 percent) who responded said they felt they did not consciously concentrate on this, but thought they probably should in the future. This 10 percent stated the more they understood their congregation the more understanding would come to the forefront in the interaction. They were also concerned because just as one person might say they were a Christian did not mean it was true. Furthermore, the last man responded he could not assume what level of maturity the person might have. He was more concerned about how much control the Holy Spirit had within their life. We pray for that to happen in all our churches today.

4th Question – Do you have any idea of what you might learn about the process or if could you observe the two natures of man in communication and which one is more prevalent? What might you expect in return if you understood the process?

Percentages for this question were impossible to determine as the answers were different for just about every pastor. The answers to this question were varied as much as the men who answered. Some men quoted scripture but never explained the context or application of the supported scripture to how it interacts with the process (which again might have taken too much time out of their day). A few responded by wanting to know more about how to do so in the future. Some responded by stating their interest in how the spiritual development (submission to the Holy Spirit's presence) of the person might affect the interactional process as each encounter occurs. Last, one responded he would be better by understanding this process and would learn how to effectively communicate with his church. This way he could help people to grow to all God wanted them to become.

So you see, there is great variance in the understanding and views of the topic, the way pastors view it, and how they interact. I learned one thing though. I learned this is an area that few are comfortable, let alone quite comfortable. My goal however is give you a good basic understanding of the topic, what it looks like in recognizing it, and how to begin to learn people's baseline behavior. This is so when departures are noticed, you will see and know something is wrong. Then you can use God's Word to help them in their sanctification process. We need to take the next step now into this process though. Are you still interested? Well hang on and let's continue the journey as we learn more!

CHAPTER SIX

An Approach to Nonverbal Pastoral Communication

Nonverbal Communication in the Context of Pastoral/ Parishioner Roles

After my questionnaires were collected and synthesized, I met with three pastors who expressed interest my findings. They said were not comfortable about how to interact with people in some of these areas we have discussed thus far. In one discussion with a pastor, he remarked of his ongoing concern with people who had previous criminal backgrounds and how they might safeguard their church from those who might try to take advantage of the church's mercy or giving. He stated his church had been taken advantage of in the past by such person(s) who came only with the intention of obtaining everything they could and then leaving. We all have had them haven't we? This is mostly because the person(s) as viewed them as weak instead their action of meekness to serve others. He stated his very appearance of being meek or mild mannered might have been the reason the person exploited their church. He said he was not sure this would have changed the whole situation in general, but it might have allowed him better insight into the motive of the person who took advantage of the church. He wished he could have been able to understand his deceptive behavior. I explained to him how tough this might have been without spending time to get to know the person and establish baseline behavior. Let's face it, there are some people who can never blink an eye and still lie to your face with no effort at all.

Within the two questionnaires, most of the men who were surveyed show interest but lack of understanding in the bigger picture of this topic. Some were also looking for more information on how to become better ministers for their people as a result of these questionnaires. They even asked me to bring this topic to a learning session for the Association to make pastors more aware of this field of study. This is refreshing in the preparation of this book, because I didn't want to write just because I was encouraged to do so. I really want to help you in this venture of learning.

In my summary, I found that most pastors have a reasonable understanding of the nonverbal communication process in day to day interaction. Many pastors do not understand it in detail or how to decipher what is a connective nonverbal behavior and what is not. They felt their understanding could always grow, but have never taken the time to study this field in detail. It is apparent that the depth of this study is new to many as result of the answers which were progressively shorter in nature throughout my progression on previous surveyed questions. I noticed that as the questions progressed, pastors nonverbally communicated their lack of understanding by shorter answers toward the end of Questionnaire Two. The questions from passages in 1 Timothy 3 have also helped me come to the conclusion that pastors understand their calling requirements from these passages, but seldom understand the importance of nonverbal communication within that passage. Most men understood the dual nature of man, however never connected the dots with how to integrate these qualifiers from scripture to the interactional process with their people. I have to admit as well that I too didn't totally understand its implications when I began the research for my project. Now I understand God's Word has a lot to say about how we are to interact; especially in the nonverbal world.

Because surveyed men have admitted to deficiencies in nonverbal communication, they must also understand how the context of spiritual engagement is also important. To assist you in understanding the role of each of us within the nonverbal interaction, the spiritual nature of the interaction has to be addressed. Each of these mandates from 1 Timothy 3 will be discussed in the coming pages which will help you understand your biblical requirements are not only part of your calling, but your daily nature in this spiritual interaction.

Since you are the normally the professional example in the interaction for spiritual growth, development and counsel of the person, your role is very important. Your role is to care for the flock by, feeding it, teaching it, and rendering aid whenever needed by guarding them when trouble arises so that no harm will come to them (or at least trying to prevent it). This interaction will also help you to understand your people better and determine whether there is a spiritual problem. It is because of this type of spiritual interaction that the exchange between Christians is quite different than secular models we looked at in the earlier chapters.

Your duty is to be the godly example to your people. I don't think there is any argument here from any of us. We are called to be the example to God's people and let's face it; everyone expects it in the real world. You are held to a higher account in God's and man's eyes (James 3:1). On the other hand the parishioner must be able to trust you on a level that honest and sincere interaction occurs. When this occurs, Christians will grow to what Christ expects in their life. When this occurs your flock will know you intimately and bond with you as they seek care and direction from God. They must learn to know you so well that when you show genuine pastoral care, they will follow you as you follow Christ. This is where trust and relationships begin. Unfortunately, over the years I have found that many pastors have been hurt by many of their people who they trusted and never engage their people in a way that these relationships occur. I would say to you if you are in this mindset to consider the example of Jesus. He picked twelve men, knowing that one would betray Him, and yet He still cared for him. I understand that in any relationship building process there is risk, but we must be willing to take that risk in faith for God's Kingdom and glory.

The Two Natures of the Redeemed Which Still Exist

To add another element you must be concerned about is the element of the spiritual identity with fellow believers in Christ. You must also be aware of the spiritual indications of trouble, concern or other weaknesses which may be hidden in the shadows of their life. Since you are communicating with a redeemed person who still exhibits sin at times (the sin nature) you must understand the implications and potential actions which could signal conflict or concern within the person's core.

Paul as one of the predominant writers of the New Testament struggled too with these natures by testifying;

> "For I know that in me (that is, in my flesh,) dwelleth no good thing: for to will is present with me; but how to perform that which is good I find not. For the good that I would I do not: but the evil which I would not, that I do." (Romans 7:18-19, KJV)

We have to understand that these two presences are constantly competing for the core of the individual and bear discernment. Discernment doesn't come over night though. Kenneth Foster explains the importance of discernment and how it grows over time;

> "Discernment is a godly spiritual perception that enables one to make more incisive observations over given data or phenomena. Discernment, theologically speaking, is the God given ability to stand back from the vents in the lives of people and perceive the direction in which hidden realities may be taking them. Christians, by virtue of their growing faith, understand and perceive more as they mature in Jesus Christ."[48]

If your people do not understand what exists within their inner man, they cannot address it for change. This requires your discernment and maturity from the beginning of the interaction. It is your duty to help the person to explore himself to his core and determine how he can effect change

---

[48] Kenneth Neill Foster, *Discernment, the Powers and Spirit Speaking* (Doctor of Philosophy diss., Fuller Theological Seminary, 1988), 17.

within his soul. To do this, you must have the ability to teach or instruct the person in a biblical process which will effect change. Remember, you are the example and the one they will be coming to for help. This only comes after you have made a decisive conclusion of the condition of their heart, and it only happens prior to an inspection. The latter must come first.

Dr. Ron Hawkins of Liberty Baptist Theological Seminary stated in one of his Doctoral Seminary lectures the importance of the Christian to possess their soul properly. He stated every Christian should have some sort of plan to determine the possession of their soul for glory of God. He states his personal vision for a good start to this is to bring;

> "The possession of the soul through the power of the Holy Spirit under the authority of the Word of God within a community of accountability for the purpose of the imitation of Christ."[49]

Dr. Hawkins explains the need for all Christians to understand the need to develop their soul in the imitation of Christ. This means the believer needs to understand what affects the soul and how to effect change. Let's face it, most people don't. You must be the instrument by which you can help develop the fellow believer in this area. You become a part of the "community" (as stated by Dr. Hawkins in his plan) for the believer. Dr. Hawkins further explains the way this person can begin to affect change with some preliminary advice and actions which need to be taken:

1. We need to possess our soul for the imitation of Christ.
2. There must be a commitment to the Holy Spirit for the possession of the soul.
3. We need the authority of the church (the main reason for the gathering of the body is to encourage love and good works, not the preaching of the word of God).[50]

---

[49] Ron Hawkins, *COUN 852, Growth and Development of the Contemporary Minister* (Liberty Baptist Seminary, May 24, 2011).
[50] Ibid, May, 24, 2011.

Dr. Hawkins states there is a need to understand how to feed the core of the person with the right and /or goodly things; otherwise the old nature will begin to prevail in this person's life. The old adage of "what is in the heart comes out of the mouth" will become evident if these areas are not addressed properly. This is also true with the *actions* of the Christian as it is fed by the core. Therefore, you must have a good understanding of the two natures which exist within people. We must also help the person we are interacting to understand the proper course his life should be upon and how to find it. We must also be able to help the person in a direction which will foster the positive development of the inner core. By doing this we help the person understand the forces which exist around each person and how they affect their life.

Finally, Dr. Hawkins gave a great illustration by his use of concentric circles and how each affect the believer's life. This illustration will help you understand the believer and how forces within and without affect his behavior and development in the Christian life.

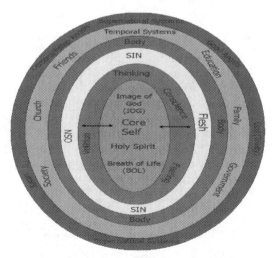

Dr. Ron Hawkins, COUN 852, Growth and Development of the Contemporary Minister "Liberty Baptist Seminary, May 24, 2011", Figure 2.

Figure 2. Concentric Circles of Influence

Within each of the circles from the inside center area (core self), each of the concentric circles outside of the core come the thoughts, feelings, etc. of each person. Each circle within this figure exerts influence upon the believer. The circle labeled as OSN (Old Sin Nature), Sin, and Flesh has other circles that are influencing its behavior as well. The thoughts, feelings, etc. circle represents where the inner life and the outer life of a believer begin. From the circles outside this area are the influences which affect the believer's life. As the influences on the outside force inward, they affect the life of the believer and determine how the person will react. This should give you a good understanding of how many affects are competing in our daily life. Let's not be naïve either, they are competing for our attention as well. On any given day, we too can react improperly when these are out of balance.

During encounters you have to be aware of indicators in your people's nonverbal behavior which may signal deeper spiritual problems which are being affected by these outside influences. This will also allow you to determine if the old nature or outside influences are oppressing the person for their possession of the soul. These influences can cause the person to become depressed, manipulate the interaction, or possibly exhibit signs of deception. When you can help the person determine what inner problem exists, you can become a conduit in which the Holy Spirit can effect change within their life. Then we can begin to place the person, if they are willing, on a path to spiritual healthiness and happiness. Let's not also forget that this is the plan God has in place for their lives. This is a life of peace and contentedness in Christ Jesus, not conflict.

Neff indicates the importance of understanding conflict and what happens when it comes:

> "Conflict is two or more objects aggressively trying to occupy the same space at the same time."[51]

---

[51] Neff, *A Pastors Guide to Interpersonal Communication*, 137.

These two natures and influences are competing for the core of the individual affected. This means you must help the person understand the importance of *daily surrender* to the Holy Spirit's leading in their life. By this submission each day, the Holy Spirit has the freedom to reign and rule within the believer's heart. Then the core of the individual is also at peace and harmony.

John Ortberg states, "Surrender is not something we do once and get over."[52] He further illustrates this by sharing his thoughts about surrender;

> "In my life and in your life there is always the question before us, who is driving? I can have a rebellious heart, telling God to stay out of my car altogether, that I will go where I want when I want with my life. Or I can have a divided heart, keeping Jesus in the car, but driving myself, saying to him, 'I will keep this area, this pattern, this relationship under my own control. I will hang onto this grudge. I will enjoy this pleasure I get from this habit. I know you want full surrender, but I don't trust you. The problem is living with divided heart makes us miserable."[53]

Wow! How true this is in each of our lives. The most miserable Christians I know are the ones who are fighting the surrender process. About two years ago, while training in the gym, I ran into an old friend from work. He was a miserable Christian. You see, he tried living on both sides of the fence. One day, I sensed the Holy Spirit gave me a word to share with him. It was "Surrender." This wasn't easy for him to swallow being a Marine veteran. "Marines never surrender," he said. After he replied, he didn't talk to me for about six months. The next time I saw him he had been fired and lost his career. The strangest thing happened though. He had a huge smile on his face as he came up to me. He told me he thought a lot about what I said to him that day. He said, "I was mad at you for

---

[52] John Ortberg, *The Me I Want to Be* (Grand Rapids, MI: Zondervan, 2010), 66.
[53] Ibid, 66-67.

quite a while… the nerve of you saying that to me!" I said "I am sorry, but I sensed the Lord asked me to share that with you." He told me, "You were right though, and I surrendered!" He told me he was trying to lead his own life and that led him to being fired from work. He said, "When I surrendered, everything came together for my life." He told me he had now surrendered his life to Jesus and was now at peace. Glory to God! Let's just allow Him to take charge of the helm. He knows the course and the end. Dr. Elmer Towns helps us understand the importance of surrender as he relates to God's people. He states;

> "Seeking God is an action, described by a verb; the result is when a Christian has surrendered himself to God, Hence it is a noun. A Christian does not automatically surrender, because he may not know what to surrender, how to surrender, or he may not have the ability to surrender. He just cannot give up his 'sin' or 'habit,' or he cannot deny the flesh. So he prays, which is seeking God. The Christian seeks God's help to surrender, or he seeks a hidden sin or hidden Bible truth that will help him surrender. Seeking God usually comes from surrendering to Him. However, seeking and surrendering usually hopscotch. Seeking that leads to a deeper level of surrender."[54]

Therefore, I encourage you to understand how vital you are as *a part* of the person's personal spiritual development. I understand that the Holy Spirit is the conduit of change within each of us, but God has also given men like you to care for and feed His sheep. This is why it is so important that you are able to understand the *full* person and his struggles. Then you can begin to use their gifts to assist them in the direction to life in the Spirit. Your ministry to them and their submission to the Lord are imperative for them to achieve their maturity.

---

[54] Elmer Towns, *Understanding the Deeper Life* (Old Tappen, NJ: Fleming H. Revel Company, 1988), 177.

One other item you must be aware of throughout the interaction process is the example to which others depend upon for God's leadership within their lives. From many of the authors' definitions in the early chapters, each author sees the communication process as an ongoing day to day interaction between people every day. This is true as well for you; however you are always the spiritual example in the interaction process. You will be counted upon as the example as a result of each interaction. This is missing in secular communication models, but from here serve as a good model for integration of pastoral nonverbal communication in the spiritual realm with the believer.

As I said before, your responsibility is to provide a godly example during the nonverbal communication interaction. I think this will bring about the end result, which is a deeper understanding of your people who you interact. It's all for the glory of God. In secular communication, the interaction may be for the purpose of giving insight into a matter (whether right or wrong guidance). You are to be the example for truth based upon the word of God. This truth you give will foster life-giving water into the thirsty believer where it might not have been previously. It will also provide peace as the believer comes to know his God in a real and personal way. When he drinks from a fresh fountain, he will never want to return to a stagnant pool.

The United Methodist Church has some good insight into the importance of the pastoral care model. It's pretty cut and dry as they state; but so true:

> "In the Hebrew Bible, pastoral care is seen as a mandate from God to the people of God to be like good shepherds to the stranger and the less fortunate in the same way that God shepherds Israel. This is part of the covenant between God and the people and is a characteristic of what it means to be God's people. Failure to care breaks the covenant and negative consequences follow. The New Testament perspective on pastoral care is both transcendent and incarnational. The New Testament continues Old

Testament notions that caring, or love (agape), originates from God and that to love another is of God." [55]

A Scriptural Design for Ministering to Others

To produce a biblical example for you to follow in ministering to others, I want to give you some scriptures for you to review and consider. Hopefully these will help you to determine if you are truly operating within your Biblical mandate and requirement of scripture.

> *"A bishop then must be blameless, the husband of one wife, vigilant, sober, of good behaviour, given to hospitality, apt to teach..."* (1Timothy 3:2, KJV)

First of all we must recognize our ability to communicate well depends upon our behavior with people. These words penned by the Apostle Paul are nonverbal in nature since they depict his character. They speak of previous behavior which needs to be established in a pastor's life. Note how the writer speaks of being "*blameless*." This word doesn't mean you are perfect; just tried and tested over time. I don't know of any pastor who has been perfect in his ministry. I would hope we are becoming more effective and prudent in the process as we grow with the Lord. "*Vigilant*" is defined as circumspect. Circumspect means, watchful and discreet; cautious; prudent: circumspect in behavior.[56] This means we must have a discreet attitude, remaining cautious in the interaction with the person, while caring for their welfare. We must be serious or concerned about the interaction with our people or *sober* (a safe or sound mind) when approached.[57] We also must exhibit *good behavior* with a person which

---

[55] *Practicing Pastoral Counseling in the United Methodist Mode* (Quarterly Review, Volume 25, Winter 2005), 376.

[56] *Webster's Dictionary Online*, http://dictionary.reference.com/browse/circumspect (accessed December 4, 2011).

[57] *Young's Analytical Concordance of the Bible* (Peabody, MA: Hendrickson Publishers, 2005), 904.

conveys a Christ-like character. This involves a sense of us being orderly, decorous in behavior which is really just being modest in nature. This word "*good behavior*" is represented by the Greek word *kosmios*. This word is where we get our English word "heaven."[58] We must have a "heavenly minded" approach and caring attitude to all who come to us. To do otherwise causes a rift in the communication process from the onset and denies the power of Spirit of God within the believer's life to act. Your ability to be "*hospitable*" also cannot be overlooked as well. You must have the ability to make the person feel welcome. You can accomplish this by using positive nonverbal indicators which reinforce your attitude and the environment. The phrase, "*apt to teach*" is another important virtue. This phrase means to be instructive.[59] We must have the ability to bring forth knowledge when interacting with any person in the spiritual realm. Otherwise we are of no value to the one who might seek input, especially in the spiritual realm. This idea of being instructive is also associated with making the instruction realistic to the person. You know, knowledge can be a great thing, but of no value when it doesn't help the person to integrate it into their life. That's the difference between knowledge and wisdom. One is learned, another is applied. When a person can live out the instructions given by the pastor in their daily life, it's a lot easier than being confused. In order for us to teach others, we too must be teachable and growing in our faith. This is how we will become better throughout ministry and for ourselves in the future.

Another scripture which must be presented for careful examination is;

"Not given to wine, no striker, not greedy of filthy lucre, but patient, not a brawler, not covetous." (1 Timothy 3:3, KJV)

Several of the words within this scripture are also presented for your examination in your own life. The word, "*not given to*" indicates to give oneself willingly.[60] This means the following words presented with the

[58] Ibid, 84.
[59] Ibid, 47.
[60] Ibid, 397.

scripture are not to be "willingness" in our life. The first is "*wine*." I understand this context is of, excess of or given to, but more importantly being alongside of wine.[61] You can't exhibit a life which is given to anything which would weaken your body or spirit while in ministry. These acts cannot be given into "willingly." Otherwise, things like this can become strongholds in life now and in our future. The strength of your life should be the reigning presence of the Spirit of God, not some other form of influence. We have enough problems with life as it is now, we don't need to add anything else. Second, the word "*striker*" means to be a smiter, reviler, pugnacious (quarrelsome).[62] In the spirit of any of us, there should be no room for a "quarrelsome" attitude. This attitude can never add anything but trouble to the conversation from the onset. I've seen the act of being pugnacious; it tends to end in a "reaching out and touching someone" incident if it gets pushed far enough. I have actually seen incidents where two ministers in a church nearly ended up in a physical altercation as a result of being overly aggressive within a verbal disagreement. I was shocked that it also started inside the church! Additionally, you must understand that while you are listening doesn't mean you are in agreement. You're merely using all your senses in the interactional process to discern the whole truth (John 16:13). Discussion can be held at a later time to confront this if needed. It might even give you time to contemplate how to confront it wisely instead of looking to right a wrong immediately. As I get older, I take my time before responding. It has saved a lot of arguments.

Carolyn Kahn explains in her book, *Non-Verbal Communications*, the need for counselors (as well as pastors) to understand listening doesn't mean agreeing:

> "To be non-judgmental is an asset to a counselor. However, during the course of the day, the counselor hears many

---

[61] Ibid, 1058.
[62] Ibid, 941.

things, some of which he does not approve, or which arouse strong feelings in him."[63]

Sometimes your disagreement may not be worth sharing until a later time when you have complete understanding and a plan. Remember this phrase; listening does not imply agreeing.

Third; *"greedy of filthy lucre"* means a pastor is not given to (greedy of), loving silver or giving oneself to the love of these things.[64] Money can never be a motivation for us. We lead a life of faith in which the Lord provides for our needs. We all must be faithful in these things or we will be tempted in the future. These things can harm our faith for God to provide for our needs and may later to a life of self-reliance. One area I suggest as well is the "giving" or being "greedy of" getting your own way on the outcomes of conversations. In this way you can also be "greedy," and that is with your own agenda. Many times you may have an idea of what is best for the person, when in fact the opposite may be true in the end. When we do this it leads to a self-righteous attitude of what is best for the person. Let's face it, we all have figured out how to "fix" the person when they come in to talk with us; "If they would only do what we tell them!"

Sabina Ludwick cautions against doing so by adding a challenge from the following scripture verse;

> "As Galatians 5:26 warns, *'let us not be boastful, challenging one another, envying one another.'* For those who are spiritual or morally strong (Rom. 15:1), there is always the temptation of dealing with sinning brother with a self-righteous, judgmental or condemning attitude. However, spiritual pride is a great offense to God and undermines true righteousness."[65]

---

[63] Carolyn J. Kahn, *Non-Verbal Communications* (Master of Science thesis, Southern Connecticut State College, 1968), 9.
[64] Ibid, 624.
[65] Sabina Ludwick, *The Grace of God in Biblical Counseling* (Master thesis, The Master's College, 2007), 95.

Fourth, *"patient"*, means to be yielding or lenient.[66] This means to be appropriate in nature, mild in behavior, gentle in spirit, and show moderation while being patient with people. This is a good suggestion as you engage in the listening process. You can also use reflective behavior to the individual by mirroring the nonverbal behavior or nodding from time to time. Patience involves listening without interrupting the communication and allowing the person to fully express their self so that all may be understood during the process. This means we must fully engage in the interaction without interrupting. This is normally where most of us find ourselves getting into problems since we want to intercede at times to give counsel.

Madelyn Burley-Allen suggests;

> "Active listening can assist you to keep your cool, remain objective, and be empathetic to the other person's point of view."[67]

This involves yielding your silence while in the interactional process. Your time will come to interact when all has been said. Listening and hearing are two different ideas.

Michael Wilson and Brad Hoffman make it pretty clear here:

> "There's a big difference between truly listening and merely hearing. Hearing is a function of the ear; listening is a function of the soul."[68]

They also contend that *reflective listening,*

---

[66] Ibid, 734.

[67] Madelyn Burley-Allen, *Listening: The Forgotten Skill* (New York, NY: John Wiley & Sons, Inc., 1995), 126.

[68] Wilson, Michael Todd and Brad Hoffman, *Preventing Ministry Failure: A ShepherdCare Guide for Pastors, Ministers and Other Caregivers* (Downer Grove, IL: Inter Varsity Press, 2007), 201.

"Is merely listening with one additional component: using our own words to reflect back to the other person what we've heard them share."[69]

Fifth, a pastor must understand the phrase, "*not a brawler.*" This means to not fight or strike.[70] You have to be peaceable. This peace comes from within our core. This true peace is only produced from our relationship with the Lord and time spent with Him. This also produces self-confidence over time. It allows us to engage in interaction with the confidence of being able to bring an interaction which might be stressful at times, to a peaceable conclusion. It also gives us a repertoire of knowledge of scripture (through memorizing scripture) to draw from in the future. This "peace" is sensed within our core which allows us to listen without fighting. Normally, a "brawler" starts or picks a fight. Since you are the example which most people will associate a connection with God, you must be on your guard in this area. The last thing we want to do is to end up in a scuffle.

Last; the word "*not covetous*" means to be without covetousness.[71] When we are caught up in the middle of wanting of something, we are in conflict with our person of peace. The peace is no longer present since there is something competing for its own satisfaction. The soul is now in conflict for its own satisfaction and being robbed by another force at work. Think back to the Concentric Circle diagram from Dr. Hawkins. What force is pushing inward on you? You must lead a life of wanting to *give* to others, not *take* from them. When this is happening in our lives, we can't give because we are too concerned about what we want. But if we address this area we are struggling with, this attitude of self-centeredness can now be replaced by God-centeredness. A God-centeredness will always produce a life which gives to others (John 15:13). This was the life of the Lord Jesus Christ. He added eternal life to each of us who trusted upon His salvation and we should do the same for our fellow man. Value others.

Understand that your interaction is always to add value to the person

---

[69] Ibid, 205.
[70] *Young's Analytical Concordance of the Bible*, 110.
[71] Ibid, 210.

and conversation. By adding valuing the person, we open the interaction to new heights. John Maxwell explains how he learned the art of valuing others:

> "Today I see my purpose as adding value to others. It has become the focus of my life, and anyone who knows me understands how important it is to me. However, to add value to others, one must value others. I didn't do that. I was so discussed on my own agenda that I often overlooked and ignored many people. If they weren't important to my cause, they didn't get my time or attention."[72]

These are such powerful words from John Maxwell as he tells us the importance of valuing people. Our purpose is to help people as we minister to them each day and when we don't, we de-value them. I think it is incredibly important for each of us to take a look at ourselves and ask the question, "Do we add value to the people we meet with in each encounter?" Also another scary question might even be to ask ourselves, "Do we have anything of value to add to them or are we too busy to listen?"

The last scripture presented for examination to the pastor is;

> "*Not a novice, lest being lifted up with pride he fall into the condemnation of the devil.*" (1Timothy 3:6, KJV)

A "*novice*" cannot be trusted with the deeper things such as encounters with people they will become engaged. Experience is a great thing during trying times for helping people. You will encounter people who will bring things that a novice cannot address; nor will be ready to do so because of their lack. Experience is not available to the young convert either. It is developed over time with the Master. Experience is the result of careful growth in the spiritual disciplines and time with His Master. If you want

---

[72] Maxwell, *Everyone Communicates*, 34.

to read a really good book in this area, I suggest, *Conformed to His Image,* by Oswald Chambers.

Chambers gives serious insight in the importance of this aspect of the developing of our spirit and how it becomes a thing of beauty when it blossoms:

> "As we obey we find that all the power of God is at our disposal, and we too can grow in spiritual beauty. Are we humble and obedient, learning as Jesus learned, or are we hurrying into experiences we have no right to? If we have to find reason for doing what we do, we should not do it. The life of a child is one of simple obedience. We grow spiritually by obeying God through the words of Jesus being made spirit and life to us and by paying attention to where we are, not to whether we are growing or not. We grow spiritually as our Lord grew physically, by a life of simple, unobtrusive obedience. If we do not obey God's Word and pay attention to the circumstances He has engineered for us, we shall not grow in spiritual beauty, but will become lopsided; our integrity will be impaired by something of the nature of inordinate lust."[73]

You cannot have another agenda when interacting with your people. If so, we show signs of immaturity and potentially damage your personal integrity. This is why these signals or cues bear close scrutiny by you at all times during the interactional process so you won't become self-centered. This starts with listening first and foremost.

Neff notes;

---

[73] Oswald Chambers, *Conformed to His Image* (Grand Rapids, MI: Discovery House Publishers, 1996), 172.

"Most people are not nearly as good at listening as their self-perception would indicate. In the case of pastors, failing to listen can mean a failure to minister effectively."[74]

When you are a poor listener, you risk the opportunity to minister. I know many times in the past as a law enforcement officer, I was called to homes repeatedly because people could not do what was right. Then we received a call to come and straighten the problem out (until the next time). After many years of working with other officers, they would tell me that if people would just shut up and listen to them (being blunt as many are); they could fix their problems in less than 30 seconds. We too can come to these types of conclusions as well after dealing with many years in experiences in dealing with our people. We too, many times are in the triage business as police and rescue personnel.

Here's the thing, if we had an idea of what was about to be conveyed from a person and make a decision prior to hearing the full detail, we are left with only a few of the facts prior to making a decision. We must have all the facts before we can properly discern the spiritual condition of this person. If not, pride can enter into the process which could produce disastrous results by failure to listen. Ask some of the pastors I interviewed. Pride and secret agendas are some of the biggest failures in the interactional process. This is because whoever it is who exhibits this behavior wants their way. There is no other option; it is only their way. As a result, they will never have the ability to fully involve the listening and observation skills needed for people. They can't because they already made up their mind.

Kahn reiterates the danger of having agendas and reinforces what we just talked about:

"Another block to listening occurs when we form an opinion about the level and value of what will be said. We label the information ahead of time as unimportant, too

---

[74] Neff, *A Pastors Guide to Interpersonal Communication*, 91.

boring, too complex, or nothing new, and we are anxious for the speaker to get to the point."[75]

She sums what happens to the person when this occurs and how it negatively affects the person. As a result, the interaction has disappeared and the person probably won't ever seek your counsel again.

> "People resent being judged and labeled negatively, and being given no choice in deciding their own actions. Often, these words and phrases result in lack of cooperation and motivation."[76]

When bias, pride, or having one's own agenda becomes the focus, whichever party has a these issues will never concede in a situation. We too know this from our personal experiences. Sometimes we will go on for years with our own selfishness and lose the relationship we are commanded to have with God's people.

This reminds me a story which actually happened to me early in my ministry as a youth pastor. In the late 1990's I was a youth pastor at a church where I was under attack from a group of people at the church from the day I was hired. One lady wanted the position and immediately began the undermining process. The Lord was gracious during that time dealing with a first-time youth pastor. I made some mistakes along the way as any pastor does; however I was not guilty of doing anything. I wanted to see the Gospel furthered at this church. During this time the church was without a senior pastor, so that added to the problem of dealing with the people who were causing the problems. When the new pastor arrived, I was able to meet with him after a week and half (yes, a week and half) after his arrival. By then, the people who sought to undermine my ministry had long since arrived in his door to voice their complaints. When I arrived in his office that day, the pastor began to lecture me about what

[75] Burley-Allen, *Listening*, 55.
[76] Ibid, 56.

was wrong with what I was doing. The problem with this situation was I never was allowed to speak or even sit down in the office. It was a one-sided discussion (or harshly toned lecture). In in my infancy in ministry, and as a full-time law enforcement officer at the time, I listened quietly during the entire half hour lecture (one of the few wise things I did early in ministry). At the end of the berating, I asked him if he had ever given me a chance to speak concerning the situation. He said he already knew what happened and was not really interested in hearing, but grudgingly said, "Well, let's hear it!" I told him there was no need to discuss it further since he had made up his own mind already and walked out of the office. I decided shortly after that time the ministry was at a conclusion (you think?). After speaking to a godly, long tenured, and wise Christian pastor whom I deeply respected, he helped me realize I needed to *run* from this situation before my ministry was damaged for good. That senior pastor who was so cruel, a few short years later resigned. This is what happens to both sides when poor listening is coupled by a personal agenda. It nearly made me step away from ever entering ministry in the future. After all, I felt safer in law enforcement and at least I could put those who attacked me in jail! I'm just kidding, but I'm sure you too understand these situations as well. They hurt and people who go through these situations are left with permanent scars which only God can heal. Some though, carry them through their whole life, and others allow the Spirit of God to heal them and grow. God helped with mine and gave me intuition and wisdom for the future incidents I would face while in ministry.

Finally, pride leaves us open to the attack of the devil. He is against both parties in the spiritual connection. He always will be in contention against the real purpose of the interaction from the onset. Make no mistake, your enemy hates you. He will do anything he can to destroy our ministries as well in the future, so let's not give him another area of weakness he can exploit. Even Timothy warns us that our testimony is critical and we must protect it at all costs:

"Moreover he must have a good report of them which are without; lest he fall into reproach and the snare of the devil." (1Timothy 3:7, KJV)

The word *"report"* is the Greek word marturia. This word is defined by evidence given, a record, report, testimony, or witness.[77] These records, reports, testimonies or witness can be observed over time and lead to a determination of maturity in the faith. As a result of all these definitions we see, trustworthiness comes over time. We must understand the nature of humans in interaction as well since often their physical needs may be different than the psychological. John Kulp in his dissertation, *Developing Empathy and Intimacy through Communication*, discusses the importance of why we should understand human nature in interaction;

> "A second important term for understanding human nature is *sarx*. *Sarx* is a very interesting Greek word that varies in meaning from the physical skin and muscle of the body to the physiologically based psychological drives of the human mind. In the latter sense is not the same as the body, *soma*, in the Greek text, which is a neutral term that refers to the physical structures only. The *sarx*, defines as the physical desires, drives and physical needs, is important for understanding the nature of the human being. Thiselton points out; 'the flesh i.e. man's existence apart from God, has therefore a drive that is opposed to God'... and, The Believer is thus already dead in respect to the ambitions and drives that mold life apart from God." [78]

This is critical if you want to truly connect with people. When there is a high level of trust and understanding of human nature and what drives them, your people can become transparent and honest without fear of

---

[77] *Young's Analytical Concordance of the Bible*, 808.

[78] John Kulp, *Developing Empathy and Intimacy Through Communication* (DMin diss., Denver Conservative Baptist Seminary, 2003), 30-31.

judgment or embarrassment. Trust from the person who interacts with you will become more evident. This will be noticed in the areas of spacial distance, proximity, and other facial and body language indicators. This person will feel valued and will be more honest with you. Many times great things happen when they do.

Larry Crabb speaks of the importance of your need to value and love each person;

> "There is a wonderful energy in each of our hearts, placed so deeply in us by the Holy Spirit that no failure or heartbreak can dislodge it. Our spirits are *alive* with the actual life of Christ. But they need to vivified, to be aroused, nourished, believed in, valued and invigorated."[79]

In addition, we have to realize our personal witness has a bearing on the outcome with others in ministry since they will be watching our behavior. I know I watched my pastors for many years and tried to mold my life by some of the standards I saw them living out in their lives. Recognize that this may even determine to what level of interaction occurs in the future between you and them too. They are watching us.

As a result, we have a duty to determine spiritual influences which affect the interactional process. To do this; you must be aware of how to view nonverbal behavior, interpret it, determining core' influence, and understand your role as the example. When these attributes from the previous scriptures we looked at are culminated in your life, the person you encounter will feel more comfortable and reflect nonverbal identification. This will affirm or *mirror* the individual's behavior back to you. That's always a good thing when it happens. It's also very satisfying when you see it actually working. It is also good feedback that is readily available.

I believe in the importance of each of these areas and believe after careful examination you will be better equipped to recognize nonverbal indicator.

---

[79] Larry Crabb, *Connecting: Healing for Ourselves and our Relationships* (Nashville, TN: Thomas Nelson, 2005), 185.

You will learn to filter each through a synthesis process by which behavior is observed and understood. This will help you to gain a basic understanding of the received messages or cues which lie in the area of nonverbal communication. You will also have a clear understanding of what can be relied upon and what cannot. This way you can discard those things that have no meaning. Then you can make an informed decision on how to proceed.

The sad statement from Wilhelm Hofmann, Tobias Gschwendner and Manfred Schmitt is unfortunately seen most every day:

> "We conclude that people have a 'blind spot' with respect to the nonverbal behavioral manifestations of their unconscious selves, even though neutral observers may readily detect and utilize this information for dispositional inferences."[80]

Second, I believe you will understand the two natures which co-exist within the believer. In doing so, you will also be able to determine which forces are at work within the person. As a result we will be able to bring good counsel to the person who is seeking input and offer the help they need. Please remember this; while secular studies of nonverbal behavior look at the outside of the person to determine what is trying to be conveyed, you must be willing to determine what is also occurring within the person. This is the core. This observation is critical while interacting with those who have the Holy Spirit's presence.

Some of the previous definitional material above mentioned deals with attractiveness (such as the study of the physical body, including the face). The pastor must be more concerned about the core of the individual as the outward appearance. The beauty of what is at heart here is the presence of the Holy Spirit. This core is made up of the soul and the spirit, apart from the body. As a result, the body must not always be depended upon while dealing with spiritual conditions. Both spiritual and physical influences

---

[80] Wilhelm Hofmann, Tobias Gschwendner and Manfred Schmitt, *The Road to the Unconscious Self Not Taken*, European Journal of Personality Eur. J. Pers. 23 (2009): 343.

need to be evaluated alongside each other. Gregory Boyd and Paul Eddy recognize the need to understand the difference. They see two interactional forces at work within the believer:

> "And John prays for all to go well with his readers so "that [they] may be in good health [i. e., body], just as it is well with [their} soul" (3 John 2). Passages such as these suggest that the physical and spiritual aspects of human beings are two fundamentally distinct realities."[81]

The simple facts of scripture assert the need to understand the cause and effect of the spirit in regards to how it affects the body. If a person is exhibiting some physical effects of sickness, it could be attributed to an inner spiritual problem. This spiritual problem could be a lack of faith, relationship and / or lack of dependence in the things of God in their present condition. Illnesses could be a result of stresses which can commonly affect the physical body. At the heart of the spiritual problem which is contained within the core, inward negative effects begin to manifest in the outward body's physical condition. Dr. Richard Swenson (a medical Christian doctor) provides some helpful insight into the balance of life for the Christian. That balance though can cause some serious problems over time when they are unaddressed.

He states;

> "We cannot achieve balance by stacking our priorities one on top of another, even though this is a common practice."[82]

Richard Swenson refers to the condition of overload in the human realm. This overload is a result of trying to put too many things in a person's life each day with no ability to control them. We all do it too. We

---

[81] Gregory A. Boyd and Paul R. Eddy, *Across the Spectrum* (Grand Rapids, MI: Baker Academic, 2007), 90.
[82] Richard Swenson, *Margin* (Colorado Springs, CO: NavPress, 2004), 188.

keep adding things to do on a life that is already too hectic and busy. He calls this "Marginless living."

Although God many times takes the back seat in a lot of lives in the real world, you must remind the believer of his commitment to Christ. His help in this world is the key to their happiness. Let's face it; a life without Christ's involvement is depressing. When we wander from God we find ourselves just drudging through another day. When we are in sweet fellowship with God, life is wonderful. We get to watch Him work each day and anticipate what He is going to do.

Dr. Swenson goes on to advise us that it is better to think of God as central to everything and then build outward from that point. He is the center of our life.

> "We do not love God, then spouse, then children, then self, then church. We love God, spouse, children, self, and church all at the same time. Similarly, we do not love God 100 percent, spouse 95 percent, children 90 percent, church 80 percent. God's standard requires that we love them all the time."[83]

His point specific to this thought is the importance that God is the central focus of everything. Submission to your people comes only when you are rightly related to God. You can give to people after being rightly related with the Master. It is also interesting to note how Dr. Swenson focuses from the inside-out. This is where we must begin when interacting with people. This is why the view of the core (figure 2) of the individual is so important in the life of every believer. Remember, secular studies focus on the outward. We are looking inward.

Third, I believe this field of study will help you understand you are always the example to those who come for counsel. We must understand the role as mentioned above through scripture and the qualifications. These qualifications might be important for *how* pastors are selected initially;

---

[83] Ibid, 188

however each qualification is just as important in the area of nonverbal interaction or counseling for people in a *daily* setting. If you carefully observe each of the previous scriptures, you will see the importance of each criterion for spiritual nonverbal interaction. God made no mistake when He listed the Bible's qualifications of the pastor. God doesn't make mistakes. Each requirement makes us a good candidate to engage people on the level God expects. As a result, we follow the calling and qualifications for being a minister of the gospel. All while using the scriptures for the purpose they were intended.

In order to successfully communicate in a ministry environment, you must be able to understand previously mentioned definitions, methods of secular nonverbal, and blend them with biblical requirements as recorded in 1 Timothy 3:1-7. The previous areas in secular nonverbal communication definitions provide a good understanding of the basics. The biblical mandate will need to become integrated if you want to communicate in the spiritual realm.

So now we come to how we go about these interactions. It's getting ready to become practical and I encourage you to prayerfully consider the next pages.

CHAPTER SEVEN

Nonverbal Communication Application

In order to put all this together, I have developed a step system based on the research conducted in nonverbal communication. Each area will allow you to move along a systematic approach before, during, and after the nonverbal interaction. The approach you will use *before* the interaction will help to set the tone of the environment, and maximize the encounter. These areas will contain the things which will be important before contact. Then you will understand how scriptural and secular nonverbal methods can be implemented together to understand what nonverbal communication looks like when it is happening. The approach *during* the interaction will help you to determine whether connecting with the individual is occurring in an effective way. This is observed by the person's baseline indicators from the onset and observing changes or deviations in behavior throughout the encounter. Baseline indicators will allow you to collect vital information from the onset. Then you will know whether or not the encounter will be productive for both parties involved. It will also allow a good *read* of the person. Finally, you will be able to determine whether the meeting provided a determined goal *after* the interaction. This will determine if a follow up meeting needs to be held to sort out any unclear information. You will also to take a look at any signs or signals which may have inadvertently been sent to the recipient to help you to become a better communicator in the future. It will also allow you to understand signals they may be sending that were not understood. Since isolating a few nonverbal cues can lead to misunderstanding between the two parties, it is important for you to use all your senses to determine what is being conveyed. If not;

"The common practice of isolating nonverbal cues from any features of context may have the unintended effect of obscuring the natural complexity vital to both theory and practice."[84]

So, let's get started with understanding each area and how to go about each section of *before*, *during*, and *after* the interaction. My hope is that the following areas will help you to develop a natural flow in the interactional process.

Before the Interaction

The physical environment will have a great influence in which you interact in relation to people. As you prepare for the time to meet you must determine what type of setting will be the most beneficial to the person in the interaction. Whenever possible, try to set the tone for the interaction and provide a healthy and conducive environment. This environment can be governed by several things which are within your control or can be determined by simple changes which can be made. Sometimes not everything is practical to change just for a meeting. This environment however must produce a place in which the person you interact will feel at their maximum level of comfort. This will allow a baseline of standard or normal behavior for the person you are interacting. The areas within secular nonverbal communication learning will be important for you to consider prior to interaction with people. You may want to go back and review any areas we discussed earlier to review how to make some changes.

Lighting will be important within the physical realm since it will determine what level of engagement is expected and conveyed to the person. If you want to display a task-related encounter, you would be wise to select one that has a maximum amount of light to keep the interaction clear or on target. Otherwise you may find yourself with someone who becomes frustrated without adequate light to see the project or intended goal. This could be problematic if not enough light to view documents or other items which might need to be clearly seen. Lower lighted areas normally convey a

[84] Joseph Cesario and Tory E. Higgins, *Making Message Recipients, Feel Right*, Association for Psychological Science, Volume 19, Number 5 (2008): 417.

more intimate setting. This setting would allow nonverbal communication in a quiet place where sharing might be more conducive or effective. It might also allow the person to feel more at ease when tough areas are mentioned which would cause significant embarrassment (hence a chance to hide the reddening of the face). This is why many sanctuaries are dimly lit during times of worship and communion. It allows the people of God to search their hearts prior to engaging. It is set in an environment of intimacy with God. Many coffee shops also use lower lighting to convey more relaxed environments for casual interactions. This removes the formality of the environment, but it does bring one thing to mind. Why then are so many young people engaging in study groups within coffee shops? I think it is mainly because they have a relaxed environment where they can study, rather than an older person like me who needs the light.

Temperature is also an important item to consider in any encounter. When an area is too cold the person may be apt to complete a conversation more abruptly because of the chilly un-comfortable climate and their inability to sit still because of the cold. This distracts any person from active listening since their concern is more focused on staying warm. On the other hand too much heat could cause a person to become more irritated simply because the heat is unbearable. Try standing in the sun in Florida in the summer months and see how quickly a conversation can end.

You may be wise to try to control the factor of heat especially under possibly volatile situations due to potentially harmful actions that could occur. Modern correctional settings are mandated in keeping temperatures which tend to side on colder settings (66-70 degrees Fahrenheit) to keep the potential of incidents occurring within the cell block areas. If it works for them, why wouldn't we use their formula? They spend thousands and thousands of dollars researching this, and you can learn it for free!

Your physical environment is also deemed in terms of space. You will need to determine how the space will be used and how it will be perceived in the interim by the arriving person. Space like this could affect the meeting and expectation of the individual that will lessen the interaction if they feel too cramped or too far away from the other person. Space can dictate the area of where immediacy of seating will be without having to ask where to sit. Adam Kendon provides an interesting comment on space and how it will affect the individual meeting;

> "There must be some way in which the behaving organism can distinguish between the space that is presently its use-space, and other space, which is irrelevant. This is because any mine of activity that an organism engages in involves a highly selective relationship between the acts in which it engages and the information from the environment that, in some way or the other, is being used in guiding these acts. Now an organism can actively select out what is relevant from what is irrelevant and so, in terms of where it can be seen to pay attention and in differentiate its present use-space from irrelevant space."[85]

When a person can differentiate what is "fair game" to sit in the space provided it will help both parties to know the boundaries of space from the onset. It will also give you an idea of what the personality of the person may be like. For instance, you may select a table in a room with chairs at each end of the table and leave your personal belongings at the head of the table to communicate leadership in the interaction if it is determined to be a task oriented or authority led interaction. On the other hand you may allow the person who arrives to take a seating position first which may be at the head of the table. This might give you an idea of the potential of the encounter as to whether the person will try to take authority or even display a passive aggressive behavior in the coming minutes. Be careful though, their seating might also be a position where they are used to sitting based upon their work experience or responsibility. This is why it is so important to not cue in on one particular action.

Personal privacy is also important if disclosure is needed in the interaction. If you want to convey trust you would be wise to change an environment in which privacy could allow others "listening in" on the

---

[85] Adam Kendon, *Spacing and Orientation in Co-Present Interaction* (2010), 1.

conversation. Sounds like common sense right? You would be surprised how many times this is violated in meetings. In other situations, some might feel more comfortable in high levels of noise since there may be no chance of others hearing, unless the level of noise dissipates suddenly. If one has to talk too loud during a high noise encounter, others might hear them when the noise lowers suddenly. If you are not sure how to plan, be wise to side in regard of maintaining solitude. This is because noise and others around us will affect the ability to hear effectively in conversation. This also reduces or causes less effective communication since a person might continuously look up to see if anyone might be listening or passing by. It can also be frustrating at times in the interaction if the selection is not well planned. Every one of us is well aware of our phones which ring constantly. Before the interaction, advise your secretary that you will be in a closed meeting and not taking calls. That also means silencing your own. To take a phone call during an interaction belittles the person and devalues them. Be wise and observe these practices to maintain respect for the person's time as John Maxwell said earlier. By taking these steps you will show genuine concern nonverbally to the person of scriptural *soberness* (serious attitude) with the person's time.

You can decide as to whether or not a door may remain open or not to the room which has been determined for the interaction. This will also depend on the level of engagement and sex engaged in the interaction. Obviously, we would have another female or witness in the room while interacting with females to *"avoid all appearances of evil"* (1 Thessalonians 5:22, KJV). Discernment is important at these times and needs to be wisely planned if possible. If not, terrible implications could occur to one or both parties involved as a result of the interaction or in the future. A lot of pastors' ministries have ended in ruin as result of poor planning in this area. It is avoidable up front, so use good common sense. When considering the Christian environment with a person, it is just as important if not more.

The common thread of the interaction (Jesus Christ) needs to be understood as well. Dieter Jagnow mentions the importance of this environment in his thesis by saying;

"A Christian congregation, pastor and members share the same Savior, faith, hope, and belong to the same body of Christ. Pastor and members are a 'community,' the community of saints."[86]

Furthermore he asserts;

"The Christian fellowship, in an ultimate sense, the relationship between the pastor and counselee is founded upon God and not upon each other."[87]

This unity of faith is critical in your encounters with God's people since the presence of God exists within the interaction, especially in confrontational matters (Matt 18:20). This action is witnessed by both human parties and by the presence of the Holy Spirit. It is because of this factor you should be aware of how scripture gives good insight into how important the pastor's calling is not only initiated, but becomes an ongoing part of daily life. Consider the following;

"A bishop then must be... of good behaviour..." (1Timothy 3:2, KJV)

One of the first areas the pastor must be aware of from the onset is his responsibility of *"good behavior"* (*kosmios*) as stated above. The translated word *good behavior* means to be orderly, decorous, of good behaviour, and modest.[88] If you want to become highly effective, you must understand your responsibility to be organized within your own life. This means having the ability to respect every person's time. This comes when we are organized in our daily life. You must have a life which is organized to keep it from being chaotic or unbalanced. No interaction with people can be haphazard,

[86] Dieter Joel Jagnow, *Communication Principles in Pastoral Counseling* (Master thesis, Concordia Seminary, 1993), 95.
[87] Ibid, 65-96.
[88] *Young's Analytical Concordance of the Bible*, 84.

especially when it comes to the life of a believer. This behavior is important since it relates to your daily inner life and relationship with the Lord. Our Lord would not have us to enter into His presence haphazardly, but with preparedness, and respect to Him. This should serve as a good example as well with people. Although the Lord has the ability to answer as quickly as we can ask questions, this is not true for us in every circumstance. This is why you must be prepared in your daily life through the discipline of reading scripture, meditation, and prayer. This way we can be a wellspring of life to those around us each day as we meet with the Master. This should be the attitude with people. Consider Oswald Chambers' encouraging words and the reward that is awaiting each of us:

> "The saints who satisfy the heart of Jesus are the imperial people of God forever; nothing deflects them, they are super-conquerors, and in the future they will be side-by-side with Jesus."[89]

Since the meaning above is also described as a life of modesty, we are not to elevate self above others. The life of modesty is one which recognizes a spirit of humility with each believer and our ability to minister. It is not a haughty or boisterous lifestyle. Otherwise we become prideful and discount the Person that exists within the fellow believer. Let's not disrespect the presence of God within the believer and grieve Him. This *kosmios* attitude is to one of a heavenly minded approach.

> *"Moreover he must have a good report of them which are without..."* (1Timothy 3:7, KJV)

In our life many aspects of this verse can be necessary to be all God expects in His calling. A "good report" is necessary of a pastor for his qualifications, but more importantly the ongoing future ministry. This good report (*marturia*) is defined as evidence given, record, report,

---

[89] Chambers, *Conformed to His Image*, 219.

testimony, or witness.[90] Our life's manifestation of a good report should be seen over time. This manifestation does not come overnight though. It can many times become ruined within a few minutes due to a poor decision that could affect ministry in the future. With this said, we will be noted of a "good report" over time in which our testimony has become solidified through the test of time, growing in the Lord Jesus Christ. Over time others will begin to speak well about us and know we are sincere to the faith. By these actions we are known for being the shepherd, not a hireling (John 10:13). This report of genuineness comes under close scrutiny over time and will be tested by others around us; however as scrutiny comes the testimony is proven genuine and remains for all to see. This area is critical for our life since every person who encounters us will already have made some decisions as to our character. This will affect the interactional process from the onset. If a person has a bad view of us from the onset, it will be manifested from the beginning of the encounter. It can determine the level of success in the interaction or willingness to follow future guidance. This *marturia* will be shown to whether we are truly mature in our faith or simply going through the motions. I hate to say it, but there are many doing this now.

> *"A bishop then must be…, given to hospitality…"* (1Timothy 3:2, KJV)

The last area of biblical concern is that of hospitality to others around us. The word "hospitality" (*philoxenos*) means fond of guests, hospitable, lover of or use of hospitality.[91] You must lead a life in which you love others around you. This applies to strangers as well. If you don't like people in general, you will find yourself in trouble from the onset of ministry. As one who is given the task of care for others you will be a miserable person. When we love people, our expression of love will be apparent from the beginning of the encounter. People around you will be able to tell if you

---

[90] *Young's Analytical Concordance of the Bible*, 808.
[91] Ibid, 492.

truly love people. This comes even after observing your behavior in a very short period of time. Often times, we do not have a great trust for people over time since we have been hurt by so many over years of ministry. This mandate is one that can only be proven consistent over time through the power of the Holy Spirit. As you grow in your knowledge and reliance upon the Lord, you understand the value God places upon each life. This should encourage us to love people the way Jesus loved the church. Jesus saw the image of God within every person He interacted with throughout His ministry and we would be wise to follow this same example He set for each of us.

These areas of scriptural nonverbal preparation are important if you want to be prepared to interact with his people. Although much of these areas discuss nonverbal character, you must understand your influence upon people will many times be understood prior to the encounter. Therefore it is imperative for you to determine the value people will place upon the interaction *before* it occurs. This way you understand what level of engagement will come when you meet with them and correct any misunderstandings along the way.

Application of Nonverbal Principles during the Interaction

To understand the encounter of the pastor to people, we must understand from the beginning of the interaction we will express different physical cues which will nonverbally communicate to others. In this section we will look at both sides of the interaction and evaluate them, while giving some suggestions to assist you in determining behavior and establishing baseline behaviors in the interactional process.

Upon our initial interaction, both parties will collect a huge amount of information about each other. Some information will be known prior to the encounter and much more following the first few minutes of the interaction. It is therefore imperative we understand this from the onset of the interaction. Unfortunately some people determine what they think about others by simply looking on the outside of the person, not the inside where it counts the most. Burgoon, Guerrero and Floyd state how many though, never get it right because they are too busy looking at just the outside of a person:

> "There are various forms of personal beauty. Inner beauty refers to the qualities such as being honest, hair, friendly and empathetic. Outer beauty, on the other hand refers to how people look based on physical characteristics such as facial structure, height, weight and coloring. Although people often perceive that individuals who are outwardly beautiful are also inwardly beautiful, sometimes, as the saying goes, appearances can be deceiving. Yet right or wrong, people often place considerable weight on first impressions, which are largely a function of how people look."[92]

In my experience, I had many encounters in the interim of ministry which distorted some of the older congregational church I served. Since I have a great love of weight lifting, my experience in the interim of ministry had some misperceptions about my behavior because of the interest in this field. They thought I was just a gym rat. Over time, I had time to interact with those around me who weren't sure how to take me in the interim. Eventually they learned that I loved God, my family, humor, life, and loved to workout at the gym with my friends. On a side note though, the gym also kept me in peak condition from being potentially hurt in my previous career. Over a short period of time the congregation determined I was not who they initially perceived me. They also understood my love and passion for the Lord through the many relationships that began to grow and culminate over the years. It is funny how I ended up having a few people join me in training at the gym! They learned that while we trained at the gym, we used a lot of the time for fellowship and building relationships with others around us. It gave us time to share the Gospel in the process with those who had never entered a church. As I get older

---

[92] Burgoon, Guerrero, and Floyd, *Nonverbal Communication*, 80.

though, it would appear that the time of fellowship is growing more and more and less training is occurring. We often use the scripture to defend ourselves; "For bodily exercise profiteth little: but godliness is profitable unto all things, having promise of the life that now is, and of that which is to come." (1 Timothy 4:8, KJV) This is our excuse to talk about the Lord and train less.

On the other hand, you have to be careful not to judge others based upon their physical appearances. To do so demeans the person from the onset and offsets a correct *read*. Some indicators in the physical realm are sometimes good indicators, but with the use of multiple identifiers it will help us to understand the person during the initial contact. In fact these types of determinations sometimes can be taken from distances away from the person without ever coming into proximity of the person. The observations by you must be held close enough to determine if there are other indicators which might signal trouble when the person comes closer as well. A study conducted by Frazer Smith and Philippe Sehyns revealed an interesting thought that space is important to determining what can be understood when in closer proximity;

> "The psychophysical data reveal a gradient of recognition proceeding as follows: sadness, anger, fear, disgust, surprise, and happiness. That sadness is poorly recognized is not surprising, because there is no obvious survival benefit to detect it from far away. It is more surprising that anger, a signal conveying threat, and fear, a signal conveying potential danger, are both poorly recognized across a range of viewing distances."[93]

What is interesting as well is that studies show spacial distance for the average American in general conversation is about three feet. As the relationship grows closer, the distance also becomes closer. This tells us a lot

---

[93] Fraser W. Smith and Philippe G. Schyns, *Smile Through Your Fear and Sadness Transmitting and Identifying Facial Expression Signals Over a Range of Viewing Distances*, Psychology Science, Volume 20 (November 10, 2009): 1207.

about spacial distance, as the closer we are to someone physically, the closer we show our relationship. On the other hand, this too can become a danger signal to those who violate these distances when there is no close relationship. Most Americans because of our culture will back up naturally if someone invades our three foot personal space if they are not in our "trust zone." Remember though; other cultures have differences in spatial distances.

Smell is also interesting physical characteristic that can help you in any encounter. A sense of smell can help you understand whether the person has recently come from outside after a hot day at work. You might learn this meeting was important enough for them to come immediately after work. On the other hand, the person could be unaware of their lack of bathing practices due to a deep depression or illness. Sometimes a person may have time to go home and bathe, then meet. This may convey his respect by appearing his best before the interaction. On the other hand it could allow the person to simply *appear* to be cloak the dirt later being examined. We are aware of people each week that come to church looking very nice but are filthy inside. This is why congruency is important and will be discussed.

Since the physical body can emanate many odors which people may or not have knowledge, you would be wise to cast off those which do not appear as if they have value. For instance, if a person has bad breath, you would understand it may no implication to the meaning of the smell or a cause for the interaction. It may be a person's medical condition or illness which exhibits these odors. On the other hand, smells which would be strongly present such as the smell of marijuana would be noticed within the clothing. This could be smelled whether they had been the one who actually partook of the substance or were in the same room with another. In this case you might be wise to determine other indicators such as the watery eyes that sometime are present of those who use these types of illegal substances. With these and other behaviors such as fleeting conversations or inability to stay on track in the interaction, you can determine the level of influence in the person and belay the interaction. This might be conducted later when they are in complete control of their faculties. That person may not even remember the interaction if they were intoxicated enough. Then both parties have wasted their time together which would not result in success because of the influence.

Since we normally see the face in every encounter, it would be wise for us to look at the face of individual in the interim and note its expressions. Does the person appear happy to see you at the initial greet then suddenly change toward unhappiness or uncomfortableness after becoming engaged in conversation of a delicate nature? Since the smile is one of the more difficult areas to determine genuineness, you should understand it is not always easy to do so as stated by Joseph Forgas and Rebekah East:

> "People seem able to differentiate between honest and deceptive communications at a level significantly, but only slightly above chance. There are a number of reasons why people are generally poor at detecting dishonest communications, including the fact that no simple behavioral cues exist that infallibly indicate deception."[94]

So ask yourself, is the expression consistent with the body language of happiness? Does it show signs of congruency with the rest of the body language? Knapp and Hall provide us some insight on how to understand this phenomenon of congruency:

> "A change in one behavior, such as the movement of a body part, will coincide or be coordinate with the onset of change in another behavior, such as in a phonological segment, or in some other body part. Just as speech units can be grouped together to form larger units, so can movement sweeps. A sweep of the arm or turn of the head may occur over an entire phrase of several words, but we may see movements of the face and fingers coordinated with smaller units of speech."[95]

[94] Joseph P. Forgas and Rebekah East, *How Real is that Smile?* J Nonverbal Behavior (2008): 32:158.
[95] Knapp and Hall, *Nonverbal Communication in Human Interaction*, 242.

When you begin the initial interaction with people, you must also be aware of his facial expression. Does you appear welcoming to the person? Are you happy to see the person you are ready to interact? Does your body language reinforce your facial expressions? Can anything be read into your expressions which would convey otherwise? We have to understand that many signals including our own smile can be misinterpreted or misunderstood as stated by Zara Ambadar, Jeffery Cohn and Lawrence Reed:

"We cannot say whether meanings perceived by decoders agreed with the messages intended by encoders."[96]

For example, does your smile convey his willingness to be with a family at a time of duress or is it perceived that somehow we think the situation is funny by the smile? Is that signal being received the way it was intended? What could be their response?

In my failed experiences of the past, I went to a person's home one day to bring an item. I was in hurry to go run other errands. When I arrived at a church member's home, I hurried to drop something at the door, thinking they were not home. Unaware of my hurried look upon my face and movement quickly to and from the home, the person came to the door and noted my hurried face and asked me if everything was alright. My facial appearance was obviously in congruence with body posturing and my hurried appearance. It was at this time I recognized how I was perceived (like I wanted to drop the package and run away). I had to apologize for acting so hurried. I had a lot to do that day and I was in a rush. I also had to slow down my pace and allow myself to value the person. Although I never expected the person to be home when I dropped off the item, I understood my actions and congruency led to devaluing the person. This doesn't mean we haven't in the past run from doors hoping no one was home either. We all have done it...

---

[96] Zara Ambadar, Jeffrey F. Cohn and Lawrence Ian Reed, *All Smiles are Not Created Equal*, J Nonverbal Behavior (2009): 33:31.

This brings about a realization of how we must be of *good behavior*. (1 Tim. 3:2. KJV) Folks, we have to take time to plan the interaction, not rush through it. The story above is one which was unplanned, but when there is an ability to plan we should be planned and prepared.

Two other areas which are important for us to observe are color and hair. As stated before, the importance of understanding the person we will be encountering is about observation in the interim of the interaction. Color is important to surroundings in some cases; however in this particular case the observation of color within the skin tone is discussed. When interacting within different racial settings, we must be observant of the differences in culture as well as possible bias from past encounters from maybe both sides of the interaction. This should be observed from both us and the individual. Sensitivity is the key in this area.

As with my best friend Roselle (for over 20 years), being a black bold for God gentleman, gave me a book a while back by Dr. Tony Evans entitled; *Let's Get to Know Each Other, What White And Black Need to Know About Each Other (1995)*. It helped me to understand a lot of things about his culture I was never aware of or understood. I recommend the book for you to consider in your library as well. It answered questions I never knew I knew to ask. It also gave us hours of laughing at each other's view on some things.

But remember, color can have a great effect on the skin tone as well. Persons of light complexions and changes to it can be observed fairly easily in embarrassing moments and/or times of crisis. Skin tones can also show a number of present medical problems as well. Some people who have high blood pressure exhibit a flushing of the face.

Hair is another area of concern. With the ever changing hairstyles of each period of time, you would be wise to observe changes in care and style of the hair. With this mind, you must be able to determine if the hair is neatly groomed in the interim. Then later they may signal trouble when you observe an unkempt hygiene. Another interesting thing I have noted is how women have used hair to cover bruises on the face with the change of a new hairstyle. This allows them to cover a possible abuse situation which may need recognition and address.

In my previous career, I encountered a young female who suddenly began covering her face with hair. This again was not unusual since many young women change hair appearances frequently. The young lady was a hairdresser by occupation and single mother who began dating another young man. In this case her behavior determined something significant happened to her in the last few days. When I met the young woman, she consistently angled herself in an attempt to cover her right side of her face from being seen. She positioned her body so that the left side of the body would only be seen. After moving around to the side after finishing (while the young lady tried to counter by moving again) I saw she combed her hair downward to cover the immense bruise upon her upper forehead. In addition, the hair was combed in a manner that a maximum amount of hair would also cover the laceration upon her upper scalp. After conversing with her about the incident and encouraging her to get medical help (like stitches), she later went to the emergency room and received fourteen stiches. It was only through closer observation this was noticed. This young woman later confided that she was ready to commit suicide if someone was not able to help her with the abuse which had been occurring by her boyfriend over this short period. We were able to help her with the reporting process and counseling for her emotional scars which were left from not only this abuse, but previous ones in the past.

And these types of tragedies happen every day. I cannot emphasize enough that you use your complete faculties of observation to reach people to determine what is happening in their life. It could mean the difference between life and death of an individual. Think of how much we miss each day by being in a hurry and not treating people like God's creation. Think of how many people we have left standing in the past with no help when we had the ability. I can tell you the military is good at treating men and women who serve our country like a number. After serving for six years I didn't like being treated like it either. I still don't like how they are treated after their service time ends. They truly deserve our nation's best care for their service.

CHAPTER EIGHT

Baseline Behavior

Baseline is important in the beginning of the encounter since it determines the level of trust which can be created in a short period of time. It will also determine any changes within the behavior from previous. As stated in the beginning of this book, the more time you have with the person, the better you will be able to understand them and view changes in the person's behavior. Remember, both parties are receiving and interpreting a lot about each person within the first few minutes of the interaction and it is very important to get a good "baseline" read on the person. Take into consideration that they are reading you as well and making some assumptions at that time. David McMillan in his dissertation, *The Development and Use of the McMillan Affective Relationship Scale in Measuring the Effects of Verbal Interaction and of Selected Non-Verbal Techniques of Communication on Synthesized Desirable Outcomes of Group Dynamics Procedures in Sensitivity Training*, says each person has their own standard in interpreting behavior;

> "There seems to be little doubt that unconscious non-verbalisms in communication produce significant information regarding the person. The important concept regarding the interpretation of such nonverbal information is that each person has his own personal subjective standard and his nonverbal behavior has meaning only in relation to that standard."[97]

---

[97] David O. McMillan, *The Development and Use of the McMillan Affective Relationship Scale in Measuring the Effects of Verbal Interaction and of Selected Non-Verbal Techniques of Communication on Synthesized Desirable Outcomes of Group Dynamics Procedures in Sensitivity Training* (Doctor of Philosophy diss., East Texas State University, 1971), 491.

To understand this better, you must determine from the onset whether you have been received well. You can determine the level of receptivity of the person by a number of nonverbal cues or behaviors which are seen together. These behaviors when compounded will allow you to have a fairly accurate "read" on whether you have been received well. This gives you a good start in the trust process so both parties benefit from the interaction.

Martin Remland provides a chart in analyzing behavior from a person to determine if there is "a level of involvement" by the person. His chart shows some clues to determine whether or not you are engaging in high or low involvement from the person. After a few minutes of viewing it, you can see that most of the data presented is a societal norm you are familiar.

Behavior	High Involvement	Low Involvement
Immediacy	Eye Contact Direct Body and Facial Orientation Leaning toward Close distances Open body positions Touch	Gaze Avoidance Indirect body and facial orientation Leaning away Far distances Closed body positions Absence of touch
Expressiveness	Facial expressions Vocal expressiveness Relaxed laughter	Neutral facial expressions Monotone voice Absence of laughter
Composure	Absence of nervous mannerisms Vocal relaxation Postural relaxation	Nervous mannerisms Vocal tension Postural tension
Engagement	Floor holding Positive reinforcers (head nods, smiling) High vocal energy Fluent speech Illustrative gestures	Avoidance of floor holding Absence of positive reinforcers Low vocal energy Hesitating speech Absence of illustrative gestures

Source: Data from Martin Remland, Nonverbal Communication in Everyday Life (Boston: Houghton Mifflin Company, 2003), table 3.[1]

---

[1] Remland, Nonverbal Communication in Everyday Life, 269.

Table 3. Nonverbal Indicators of Conversational Involvement

From the chart, you can see some obvious changes in behavior which might signal the level of engagement from the onset of the interaction. Although these behaviors might not be an all-inclusive way to determine the level of engagement, they provide some basic information while establishing interaction. Things which might affect the process could be things such as the person's personality or temperament. This could affect the behavior areas listed above. For instance, if a person was shy in nature, several of these indicators could signal a low level of engagement by avoiding eye contact, close distancing, lack of touch, quiet or low speech, nervous mannerisms or smiles, etc. These could be perceived as low engagement but in reality might signal personality differences than understood in the interim.

Other factors which also could affect this chart are those who see the interaction as possibly confrontational or stressful. This would affect the level of engagement from them to avoid further conflict since they are passive in nature. It also possible during these times people are receiving signals from the pastor whom can be challenging or harder to interpret. An interesting fact from Eva Krumhuber, Antony Manstead and Arvid Krappas, state women tend to have higher decoding skills than men in general.

"Women's greater sensitivity to nonverbal signs and higher decoding ability therefore suggest that women may read smile dynamics in a more fine-tuned way than men do. Consequently, they may be more likely to use the extreme poles of the rating scale."[98]

Since women generally decode better than men in smile dynamics, it would also mean there is something different about interacting with women in the nonverbal communication process. Since this difference between men and women is significantly different you should understand these possible differences. That means men may not engage as readily as women in matters of sharing in the interim, just because of their gender makeup. Jonathan Gore suggests how men and women differ in respect to interaction;

---

[98] Eva Krumhuber, Antony S. R. Manstead and Arvid Kappas, *Temporal Aspects of Facial Displays in Person and Expression Perception*, J Nonverbal Behavior (2007): 31:42.

"More specifically, men 'typically discuss topical issues such as sports, careers and politics whereas women focus on the discussion of feelings, motivations, relationships, and personal problems' In general, women are more likely to disclose private and personal information in a conversation than men, perhaps because it fosters intimacy. Others have shown that boys and men are particularly uncomfortable expressing their feelings with other males, but men are willing to disclose feelings to another man if they believe that they will be collaborating on a future project with that person."[99]

This area is vital for you to understand how a man might react in the future if the engagement is continued down the road. If the conversation begins with something he is more comfortable speaking about in the beginning you may have better success. It should also give you some confidence understanding the engagement for a female may move much quicker into sensitive areas than male. At whatever interaction, including sexual orientation, you need to set the level of engagement. This begins at the lowest risk level of engagement by talking about things such as family, friends, occupations, and other areas where the person might feel the most comfortable. In my experience I have noticed when entering the person's home, it is important to look at photos which are inside the home. These will help you determine what is important to the person and how they provide nonverbal cues of value or accomplishment.

Pictures of family, friends and animals can be good indicators of value to the person when entering their home. The way in which these pictures are displayed is also important to note as well. Psychological research has produced information that photos which are on a desk or seating areas which are facing the person convey emotional support to one behind the desk. Pictures which are displayed outward so all can see (maybe even

---

[99] Jonathan S. Gore, *The Interaction of Sex, Verbal, and Nonverbal Cues in Same-Sex First Encounters*, J Nonverbal Behavior (2009): 33:280.

hanging on walls in the home) suggest levels of accomplishment and pride. You need to observe these displays and observe what is important in the person's life. Not only are pictures important to notice, but you can also see other "trophies" which might be evident inside a person's home which would indicate their personal levels of accomplishment such as certificates, diplomas, flags, and letters from high levels of authority.

The need to determine if the interaction is going to occur within your own office setting is also being conveyed to the person who arrives. You might ask yourself in the future about your own office; "What am I sending nonverbally to the person by the appearance and decoration of my office?" It might be a good idea to design your office to send nonverbal messages for the purpose of the interaction. Do you want to convey authority? Then place certificates, diplomas, etc. in an area where they will be readily viewed. Do you want to convey compassion to people? Perhaps you might have photos in plain view which show the value of family or friends. Is the furniture situated in a manner that the interaction will be personal in nature or does it need to be conveyed as more authorative in nature? These areas are important if you want to determine whether it will positively affect the interactional process from the beginning. It will also allow you to speed the process of baseline behavior the way these arrangements are arranged.

Once the initial interaction begins and the conversation becomes more comfortable for the person over a period of minutes, you should try to transition slowly into the reason for the interaction. Once this has been established, watch for changes in behavior which would signal tension, apprehension, lying, and fear if the topic will be somewhat difficult for the person. These changes may even be exhibited by the person when lying to make the lie believable. Sharon Leal and Aldert Vrij give insight into this phenomenon;

> "As such, liars will be more inclined than truth tellers to monitor and control their demeanor so that they will appear honest to the lie detector, which should be cognitively demanding. Third, because liars do not take

credibility for granted, they may monitor the interviewer's reactions more carefully in order to assess whether they are getting away with their lie."[100]

These lies may also seem to be trivial in nature, but begin to tear down the process of integrity from the beginning of the interaction. Lies can be understood as anything;

"..from trivial, so called 'white lies' to situations in which the consequences of detected deception are grave—especially those involving the law."[101]

When these changes occur, whether internally or externally, your duty is to exhibit *soberness*, mentioned in 1 Timothy 3:2. You must help the person realize you is concerned about them and there to help in any way possible. This *soberness* must convey *passion* (by definition) for the individual to provide the care which is needed for the person's soul. Passion is an attribute which cannot be faked. It will be visible to the person you meet and shows a genuineness. Even small children can read passion in an adult. It is funny how they can even detect it from such a young age. Your interaction must convey *moderation* (by definition) in which allows the person to know you are in full control and able to assist the person in any way help is needed. When you show moderation to the person, you are exhibiting confidence and leading with the power of the Holy Spirit's assistance. This produces confidence within the person that we are there to help them. This power and confidence can only be conveyed by the Spirit's presence within the interaction and identification by the person. This helps to draw from the real power of the encounter (the Holy Spirit) which now makes the encounter a spiritual encounter. The Bible tells us that the fruits of the Spirit are;

[100] Sharon Leal and Aldert Vrij, *Blinking During and After Lying*, J Nonverbal Behavior (2008): 32:188.
[101] Gemma Warren, Elizabeth Schertler, and Peter Bull, *Detecting Deception from Emotional and Unemotional Cues*, J Nonverbal Behavior (2008): 33:59.

"Love, joy, peace, longsuffering, gentleness, goodness, faith, meekness, temperance: against such there is no law" (Galatians 5:22-23, KJV).

When these all are made manifest within the encounter, you are on the winning side of the interaction to help the person grow in their faith from the encounter. As the Holy Spirit is in the interaction, the results are true blessings from God.

Baseline will also help us to understand the real person for who they are, not how they appear to be. It will also give some clues on how to respond to the person when certain cues are viewed during the interactional process. During this time of observation, you must be willing to observe with all your senses so that other filters, prejudices, or bias do not enter while assimilating the information being sent by the person.

Another way to look at this interaction is use a monitoring skill which is known as emotional intelligence. This emotional intelligence is defined as;

> "The ability to understand, manage and utilize your emotions to meet goals and to understand the emotions of others."[102]

Emotional intelligence is also defined by Peter Salovey and John Mayer as;

> "We define emotional intelligence as the subset of social intelligence that involves the *ability to monitor one's own and others' feelings and emotions, to discriminate among them and to use this information to guide one's thinking and actions...*" [103]

Salovey and Mayer add another interesting element to the definition in

---

[102] Burgoon, Guerrero, and Floyd, *Nonverbal Communication*, 311.

[103] Peter Salovey and John D. Mayer, *Emotional Intelligence, Imagination, Cognition and Personality,* Vol. 9-3 (1989-1990): 189.

predicting future behavior as well as a result of using emotional intelligence. They call this Interpersonal Intelligence;

> "Interpersonal intelligence involves, among other things, the ability to monitor others; moods and temperaments and to enlist such knowledge into the service of predicting their future behavior."[104]

These factors may allow you to determine future behavior by monitoring current behavior; however there are many things from each person's past which prevent or limit the interactional process when it comes to listening. Madelyn Burley-Allen in her book, *Listening, The Forgotten Skill*, suggests things which affect our ability to correctly listen. When all of the things come into our life that affects us, we use them to filter what we hear based upon our past. These areas such as "memories, images from the past and future, expectations, values, beliefs, attitudes, physical environment(s), interests, strong feelings, assumptions, past experiences, and prejudices,"[105] affect interaction.

An additional method not mentioned in detail by Burley-Allen (since the book is primarily used for verbal communication study) is in observing behavior such as the listening process. You must be able to *observe* as well as listen during the period of establishing baseline behavior. Burley-Allen discusses this as a manner of understood process; however I would like clarify this area a little more. The *observation* involves using all the senses rather than use of the ears or eyes. Both are important to baseline observance; however I suggest an additional step to gain understanding of what is being conveyed in the interim. My idea is also supported by Burgoon, Guerrero, and Floyd in the realm of smell,[106] along with Salovey and Mayer in how feelings affect us:

---

[104] Ibid, 189.
[105] Burley-Allen, *Listening the Forgotten Skill: A Self-Teaching Guide*, Figure 2.3, 39.
[106] Burgoon, Guerrero, and Floyd, *Nonverbal Communication*, 108-109.

"When the pastor can listen with all his physical senses as well as his spiritual intuition, he will be better suited to determine what is occurring with the core of the individual. When the pastor is able to use his spirit to assist him in discernment of conflict within a person, he is better suited to help in a matter which can heal and bring peace to the person's soul."[107]

Again, the interaction of the Spirit's presence is the key in these interactions. If we simply use our physical senses in the interaction, we are leaving out the key factors to true Christian nonverbal interaction. If we say we can understand what is happening without the benefit of the Spirit's intuition, it leaves us with our human faculties which are at best imperfect. This risks all God intends for the life of the one whom he meets with in the interaction. Then an action could become manipulation of behavior to a desired result, rather than transformation of the Christian life. This is because we all know how quick we can get in the flesh, and we know where that leads.

The Interaction in Action

When the two people come in proximity to another, there are a number of ways the encounter begins. Martin Remland discusses different ways people initially contact each other;

"The first stage, *sighting and recognition*, occurs when we make eye contact with another person. The second stage is *distance salutation*, saying hello with a wave, eyebrow flash, nod, smile, and so forth. But our intention to engage in conversation doesn't become apparent until we enter the third stage of the greeting ritual: lowering our head and averting our gaze (to avoid staring), we *approach* the other person. A resumption of mutual gaze and smiling quickly

---

[107] Ibid, 189.

follows our initial approach. In the fourth stage, *close salutation*, we offer an open palm and engage in some type of physical contact, such a handshake, kiss or hug. The fifth and final stage of the greeting sequence, *backing off* (e.g. taking a step back, turning to the side, etc.), orients us to the conversation and creates a certain amount of distance that varies from one relationship to another."[108]

When you come in immediate contact (or *salutation* as mentioned by Remland) with the person, the normal exchange for greeting is a handshake for men. Carol Goman gives us some insight on how important the shaking of hands is and how rapport begins. She states:

"This is quickest way to establish rapport. It's also the most effective. Research shows it takes an average of three hours of continuous interaction to develop the same level of rapport that you can get with a single handshake. (Just make sure you have palm-to-palm contact and that the web of your hand touches the web of the other person's)"[109]

Women may convey the greeting somewhat different or same depending on the level of the relationship with the other. A firm handshake by any person could be a good indicator of the person's internal confidence, whereas a handshake from a timid person might be significantly lighter or limited in the level of physical contact in the handshake. A full extension of the arm can convey openness and anticipation of the interaction. An arm which is slightly extended might indicate a resistance to proximity, due to nervousness or timidity. On the other hand, the lack of interaction in contact will normally signal the disinterest or uneasiness of the individual who is meeting with you. These actions of touch are important to establish contact with people from the onset. It will also allow an initial "read" on

---

[108] Remland, *Nonverbal Communication in Everyday Life*, 261-262.
[109] Carol Kinsey Goman, *Watch Your Language*, America Society for Training and Development (August 2008): 95.

the person of the receptivity of the encounter. Discernment will need to be clearly established from the onset to determine different personality types and analyzing this "read." This is where prior prayer, asking God to give your insight and favor with the person you are about to meet.

When you come into contact with the individual, you set the tone for the interaction by your *"act of hospitality"* (1 Tim. 3:2, KJV). The goal from the onset of the interaction is to be welcoming, showing a good attitude, and having a willingness to meet with the individual by expressing nonverbal communicators such as a smile, possibly raised eyebrows as a sign of anticipation or excitement, a firm handshake or hug (depending on the depth of the relationship) to the one engaged.

After baseline behavior has been established, begin to looking for changes in behavior which are occurring within the individual as the conversation progresses into the reason for the visit. These signal possible differences as the nonverbal communication proceeds. You must observe all the indicators which signal changes. Goman also reinforces this thought as she says;

> "You need to know a person's baseline behavior under relaxed or generally stress-free conditions so that you can compare it with the expressions and gestures that appear when that person is under stress. So, when you interact with your business colleagues, notice how they look when they are relaxed and comfortable. Note their eye contact, gestures, and body postures. Knowing someone's behavioral baseline enhances your ability to spot meaningful inconsistencies."[110]

These conditions are important to the rest of the interaction, since you will need to understand what is affecting or influencing the person. When you understand what changes are being signaled, discernment comes to help the person. Again, be wise to observe all the changes, not just one

---

[110] Ibid, 95.

or two initial signals. To do so, could lead to an inconclusive baseline determination and affect readability.

When you see changes, observe those patterns which are exhibited that are not in congruence with their intended actions. When a person is being honest, normally the nonverbal indicators will exhibit congruence in their body language. On the other hand, the person who is trying to convince you verbally may not be aware that their actions do not support their mouth. This is due to inconsistencies of their nonverbal expressions. Now these changes in nonverbal behaviors should be noted. This doesn't mean later telling the person you noticed the changes. It's our observations we note and store, not share. We are there to help, not manipulate.

At this time be aware how important the nonverbal indicators are in the *Before the Meeting* section. This section includes your scriptural mandates before the meeting such as a *good report, given to hospitality, soberness, good behavior*, etc. Be aware if these traits are already in place in the person's mind from the onset. These factors will help to determine the level of disclosure in the interaction and success. Other the other hand you should be aware of misunderstandings which might have been perceived by the person. This could cause an incorrect person's *read* on you before the meeting as well. You can dispel these misunderstandings by integrating the biblical behaviors which were discussed previously to assure the person of your character and care. As I stated before, the scriptural mandates listed within 1 Timothy 3 will allow the Holy Spirit to bring peace into the meeting.

The following two sections; *The Pastor*, and *The Person* will also allow you to determine the levels of behavioral observation. Each section will provide some basic observations which are necessary for both parties. Remember, the purpose of this book is not to exhaust everything in this topic, but allow you to have a basic understanding of our study.

CHAPTER NINE

The Pastor's Nonverbal Communicators

Once the person is comfortable, your nonverbal body language must be used to help communicate genuine care for the person. As you get ready, here are a few suggestions:

1. The Eyes - Are you preoccupied with other things and are you prepared? When you are preoccupied you devalue the person from the onset. This means *never* answering telephones or doing paperwork during your time with them. As simple as these things sound, many of us are multitasking during or time with people. Even in our minds. Look in the person's eyes and acknowledge their presence. Convey a friendly welcoming attitude. Remember, you want to avoid looking into the eyes of a person for too long. You could cause the person to feel a little uneasy from the start. If our eyes are where we observe nonverbal behavior in general, we don't want to get off to the wrong start in the initial greeting.

2. The Face - Have a genuine smile. Many times the smile is the connecting factor for people when they need it. Your face should convey interest in meeting with the person. This is especially true when you don't know where the conversation is headed. Over the course of the interaction guard your facial expressions. Remember most feedback is received from your face. Your facial expressions convey interest, serious listening, and concern for the person. These facial expressions should show support throughout your time. Simple head nods or a short one word replies you are actively listening.

3. Body Posture - Sit so you convey an attentive posture. Keep good posture. It's good for posture and it shows you are interested in

listening. Correct posture even improves blood flow to the body. If you slouch consistently, you may signal disinterest or boredom. When you take a seat understand the level of the relationship you hold with the person. Use spatial distancing to interact at a desired comfort level for both of you. If you note the person move away, this is your cue you have violated their personal space. In other cases where a relationship is new, you may seat yourself near the person (within a few feet), and then allow them to move closer. This will be noticed as the level of the relationship improves. Consider personal integrity at all times of how close is too close. Otherwise this could be perceived as too intimate or familiar. Candor and good common sense must be used at these times. In some cases, I have noticed that some women prefer to move closer during the conversation. This sends a signal of increasing trust. Remember, women build relationships faster and at greater depths than men, so don't gauge the wife's engagement against the husband. In other situations, I have seen both sexes draw back during times of stress. In each of these instances a signal was sent and we need to take note of what happened that affected the change.

It is up to you at these times to help reaffirm trust with people. We are there to help. The Lord Jesus Christ has sent us to be conduits of His love to them during their time of need. As we help people, we enlist the Holy Spirit's interaction as well.

Jagnow reaffirms what we have been talking about throughout this entire chapter;

> "The pastor must show the counselee, by verbal and nonverbal language, from the beginning of the process that he is there and ready to help the counselee in his problem."[111]

4. Hand Gestures – Hand gestures are used widely in our society today; some good ones and some bad ones. Because of our cultures in the

---

[111] Jagnow, *Communication Principles in Pastoral Counseling*, 100.

world and differences let's stick to America. What one hand signal means in America might be totally different in another country. I made a few of these mistakes when I grew up in Europe as a child and an adult while serving in the military in Germany. My thumb pointed up meant something totally different in Germany, than here in the United States. So, let's stick to what we understand, or think we understand.

Here is where it can get tricky though. Do we fully understand every hand signal we see? I thought I did years ago, but now I understand that there are significant differences even within America today. This is why we must make sure we are interpreting the signals we see from people. It may even take us asking people what the hand gesture was trying to convey.

When you meet with someone, are your hand gestures inviting? A hand gesture that is open normally means a welcome or greeting. This is why the handshake shows an open hand. When the palms are facing upward with the fingers spread apart it conveys openness, sincerity, and honesty. A right hand wave, which is thought to come from the earliest times, was thought to show a greeting and show that there was no weapon in the weapon hand. So you can see how the openness of a hand indicates a number of non-offensive signals.

It is also true that when hands are facing toward the body that many times the position can be defensive or protective in nature. Think about crossed arms; palms are inward. Fists clenched are signs of aggression and firmness. When palms are facing downward, it conveys rigidity. Downward palms with the fingers straightened indicate a sense of authority or dominance. Hands that are striking downward many times indicates authorative and emphasis to a statement. Hands that are clenched together indicate uncomfortableness or nervousness. An index finger pointed with the palm down indicates authority or identification. Another way to point might be to use all fingers rather than one. This might help indicate direction without using a signal that many are familiar with as an accusation.

We also need to understand that hand signals may or may not be understood by the person. This is why we need to make certain they are being received properly. If they are not, they lead to miscommunication. Sometimes they can even be discarded for meaning completely because of their repetitive nature. We all know how some people use their hands to talk all the time, and after it can even become comical. We also realize that if these people were missing both arms or forced to put them in their pockets, they would be in a world of hurt!

Using hand gestures is a progressive art though. It takes time to communicate well with gestures as Fred Smith says:

> "You won't develop mastery of gestures quickly, but you can improve."[112]

5. Touch - The effect of touch can be used in certain circumstances which can convey care such as a touch on the shoulder or hand to convey care. You must determine if you will use it, how you will use it, and at what time. Decide if it will be used as a method of encouragement (a pat on the shoulder or upper back), healing (holding the hand of the person), symbolism (a firm grip of hands by another male to the top of the shoulder to convey care in a masculine sense), etc.

Dariusz Dolinski says even the social status of another can even encourage subordinates to fulfill requests:

> "Most often it is pointed out that touch is not only about physical, but also psychological intimacy. That is why we may perceive a person who touches us delicately as nice and friendly, which in turn will incline us to comply with their requests. An alternative interpretation, also popular in the literature on the subject, assumes that one-way touch in a social interaction is associated with the higher social status of the person who touches someone of lower social status (e. g., a teacher drawing the attention of a student, a soccer coach instructing a player before he enters the field). If the

---

[112] Fred Smith, *How to Be Heard*, Your Church (September/ October 2007): 104.

person touched by a stranger behaves, at least to a certain extent, automatically or thoughtlessly, they may react as they would typically do when touched someone of higher social status and hence may fulfill the stranger's requests or suggestions."[113]

You must also be aware since you are the example, our level of influence is extremely important. Dolinski makes this assertion in the above statement with regard to the social status of a pastor to his people. Because of pastoral influence with people, you must be aware that the extent of touch can influence people to act in a particular way. This is especially true if the trust level is strong. This sense of touch is important since it conveys *connection* of both parties. This research by Dolinski is encouraging for all of us since it gives hope that the level of care may produce something which can help the person in their daily life. It also affirms the pastoral requirement to be *"of good behavior"* (1 Tim. 3:2) to people.

This level of trust is also important in the relation of *matching.* Suzanne Jones and John Wirtz tell us:

> "For example, if both conversational partners use large amounts of touch, then behavioral matching has occurred. If one partner uses no eye contact while the other partner engages in high levels of eye contact, then no matching has occurred."[114]

This level of connecting (whether various terms used as *matching, meshing, etc.*) by terminology to people is successful when the two engage in high levels of physical contact. The same thing is true in the realm of eye contact. Jones and Wirtz tell us when only one person maintains high

---

[113] Dariusz Dolinski, *Touch, Compliance, and Homophobia*, J Nonverbal Behavior (2010): 34:180.

[114] Susanne M. Jones and John G. Wirtz, *Sad Monkey See, Monkey Do*, Communication Studies, Vol. 58, No. 1 (March 2007): 73-74.

levels of eye contact and the other is not, neither are experiencing complete connection or *matching*.

6. Learning to Discern Self - One thing to consider is our own personal problems which are going one while we are trying to help people. Since things in your life may not always be smooth, consider how to discern yourself so you can be helpful interacting. You must be able to understand yourself so you can effectively help people. Scazzero and Bird note some very important factors to understand about ourselves:

   A. Look at your personality - Do you get more energy from being with people (extrovert) or from doing tasks (introvert)? Are you more spontaneous and creative, or controlled and orderly? Are you more easy going and relaxed, or tense and anxious?

   B. Look at your season of life - Your season of life is also a God-given limit... There are times when, because of health reasons, our families need us. There are seasons of financial prosperity and times of struggle. There are times to be studying intensely and preparing. There are times for great activity. There are times to grieve a loss and wait.

   C. Look at your situation - Your life situation is also a limit. When we age physically, we find our bodies cannot do what they used to. When we are young and without much life experience, certain doors may remain closed to us. If we have a physical or emotional disability or a sickness, we may find this keeps us from going down a path we may have planned.

   D. Look at your emotional, physical, and intellectual capacities - Your emotional, physical, and intellectual capacities also are a God-given gift... When we don't respect God's limits in our lives, we will often find ourselves overextended, stressed, and exhausted.

   E. Look at your negative emotions - Anger, depression, and rage, for example, often function as oil lights in our lives, informing us that something is not right on the inside of the engine of our lives.

   F. Look at your scars and wounds from your family past - They are also God-given limits and gifts. If we will look for the hand of God moving in our family history, even in the most painful moments, we will find golden nuggets in that rocky soil. Abuse, neglect, abandonment, poverty, oppression, and so on may cause us to feel we are "behind" always trying to catch up. God sees it differently. [115]

Another area which could be important to remember is by understanding the basic types of interpersonal needs. John Swift addresses some areas which are important to understand when realizing our full potential. He notes:

"These interpersonal-need areas are inclusion, control and affection. The first interpersonal need, inclusion, refers to association between people, being excluded or included, belonging, togetherness. Self-identity is essential in understanding inclusion needs. To be understood implies that someone is interested enough in him to find out his particular characteristics. The second need is control."[116]

He further indicates the need of control by stating how control can be a negative thing as well by saying;

"The need to control another is a limitation of the other's freedom of expression. Schutz characterizes the dominant person as the 'autocrat' who is afraid that people will control him; so he does them first."[117]

Lastly he mentions:

[115] Peter Scazzero and Warren Bird, *The Emotionally Healthy Church* (Grand Rapids, MI: Zondervan, 2003), 142-143.
[116] John Swift, *Toward a Theoretical and Theological Framework for the use of Therapeutic Non-Verbal Communication Experiences in Group Pastoral Counseling* (DMin. Thesis, School of Theology at Claremount, 1969), 113.
[117] Ibid, 114.

"The third interpersonal need is affection. Affection refers to the degree of emotional ties between individuals, especially in the form of love and hate. Affection behavior differs from control behavior in that the emphasis is on emotional relationship rather than power relationship."[118]

These factors will help you to become more effective in life and to add value to others, but it begins with you. It will also allow your insight to determine if there is a level of what you can and cannot engage. These are due to things which are consuming your thoughts. You may even decide if the encounter needs someone who is professionally trained to engage in the particular topic. This is especially true if you are unqualified or unsuited to do so at the time. Become someone who has an "affection behavior" if you truly want to connect with people. If not, you need to get someone who can, or reconsider your failings in this area and consider change. As I said a while back, we can't do it all folks. God has given His body gifts, and these gifts He gave to minister to the church. Allow those who have the gifts to minister in the capacity that the Holy Spirit of God has given to them. When they do, God is glorified and people are built up.

When you have an interaction related to conflict, be sensitive as well to the needs of people. The hammer is not the only tool in the box. These areas bear close scrutiny and discernment to make sure there are no misunderstandings when it comes to conflict or adversity. As you deal with biblical conflict and adversity, you are helping the person become who they were intended.

One of my favorite authors, Charles Stanley offers some timeless wisdom in the area of adversity by saying:

"Since adversity is God's most effective tool insofar as spiritual growth is concerned, the degree to which we desire to grow spiritually corresponds to our ability to handle adversity successfully. Men or women who are only marginally

---

[118] Ibid,114-115.

interested in maturing as Christians will have a difficult time with adversity. Their tendency will be to blame God and become bitter. Instead of seeing adversity as something God is trying to do for them, they will see it as something He is doing to them. It is a matter of priority and perspective."[119]

But what does an assertive person look like? Roy Oswald shows us three types of assertive people. Many times these people are the heart of the problem or perceived to be the problem in dealing with adversity.

1. The Passive, Non-Assertive Person:
   A. denies self.
   B. is usually inhibited, hurt, and anxious.
   C. continually defers to others in making choices for his/her life and,
   D. is usually ineffective as a person and/or as a professional.
2. The Aggressive Person:
   A. enhances the self at the expense of others,
   B. tends to depreciate others,
   C. tries to decide matters for others, and
   D. normally achieves desired goals, but hurts others in the process.
3. The Assertive Person:
   A. is self-enhancing,
   B. expresses positive feeling about self,
   C. chooses for self and accepts consequences, and
   D. usually achieves goals, yet not at the expense of others.[120]

Not all these types of people are always bad as well. Each of these people can be of great benefit at times. The majority of the time dealing with these types of people need to be handled quite differently for a

---

[119] Charles Stanley, *How to Handle Adversity*, (Nashville, TN: Oliver-Nelson Books, 1989), 73.
[120] Roy M. Oswald, *Clergy Self Care: Finding a Balance for Effective Ministry* (New York, NY: Alban Institute, 1993), 174.

successful encounter. It is therefore important to note different types of temperaments in interaction.

You must be willing to deal with adversity in way in which people can grow as a result of the conflict. If not, your rapport with people can become damaged in the future. There is also a possibility of people criticizing you in the future. These times are often tough since our intent is to help rather than be attacked. Learning to deal with sorts of adversity however is important to anyone. Let's face it, all of us have been there and experienced this happen within our lives. If you are in ministry, you know exactly what I mean. The difference is how we handle it though and our responses will set the tone for the future. George Thompson and Jerry Jenkins tell us how words and how we act are super important:

> "Being criticized and responding appropriately can better than never having been noticed at all. Your demeanor and ability to choose your words carefully make all the difference."

Thompson and Jenkins give us some really good practical guidelines for taking criticism:

1. Maintain eye contact. Don't roll your eyes as if you are amazed the stupidity of the person doing the criticizing. And don't cast down your eyes either. That is a sign of resignation or defeat. The person criticizing you probably doesn't want you to wallow in self-pity. Look at the person in the eye and indicate that you're listening.

2. If you disagree, hold your tongue for the time being. If you constantly interrupt to correct an inaccuracy or plead your case, you're going to look worse... gather your thoughts first and be prepared to discuss them calmly, just try to balance the record.

3. Nod and show an open body language that says you're not only listening, but also that you're hearing and understanding. You're not necessarily agreeing, but you're getting the message.

4. Use phrases that confirm your openness to be corrected such as "Uh-huh," "Yes," "Okay," "I hear you," "I understand what you're

saying," "I'm willing," "I'll make every effort," "I'll work on that," "Thanks for pointing that out."

5. When you have the floor, use the opportunity not to only to defend yourself but also to reiterate that you welcome such input and want to learn. Insist on a follow-up meeting with a request such as "Could I check back with you to make sure I'm making progress and doing what you want?"[121]

Despite some of the responses mentioned and how they may hurt at times, it is important you have a teachable spirit. Recognize you may not always be right. This process refines us for future successes if used in the right spirit. Kevin Harney says people also have the ability to help us in decisions. During some of these times we can gain wisdom from others. He encourages you and I to understand that God placed people in our lives to help us, not always hurt:

> "Let's be honest, we don't have all of the answers. And we don't have to reinvent the wheel every time we want to go somewhere. God has placed people all around us who have a great deal to offer. I have discovered that most are more than willing to share their wisdom, expertise, and even failings if asked."[122]

The teachable spirit in your life will allow you to become the man of God you are instructed to be as you continue to grow. Let's also face the fact that we too have not arrived. Some men have forgotten that while serving in ministry. Jesus Christ is the only one I know who fits this image. As the Holy Spirit in His continuing patience is growing each of us daily (as we avail ourselves), we should thank God for His infinite patience with each one of us every day. God knows our limitations and yet chooses to use

---

[121] George J. Thompson and Jerry Jenkins, *Verbal Judo* (New York, NY: William Morrow and Company Inc., 1993), 193.
[122] Harney, Kevin. *Leadership from the Inside Out: Examining the Inner Life of a Healthy Church Leader* (Grand Rapids, MI: Zondervan, 2007), 72.

us for His people every day. It is only with that grace He extends to us. We must also extend that grace to others when trying to communicate with them daily. Remember, we are all on the same side. God's side!

In other cases you will encounter, you will also deal with people who have no desire for the things of God, nor to grow into His shaping. Although it's sad this is becoming more of a common occurrence in American society today as we drift from being "One Nation under God." Man continues to embrace this secular-humanistic way of thinking. It is also beginning to show in the collapse of moral God-centered society.

Where were we? Leave the door open for future conversations when the person may come back into the fold. We never know what the future holds for these people. We must leave the door open to opportunities with them in the future. Even if we still disagree with them in their current direction, it still leaves the communication avenue open for possible future life changes. This is true in my personal experience.

I know a man in his thirties who checks in to see how things are with the church and I. He left the church about two years ago after moving to a different city and going through a divorce because of the spouse's drug addiction. It was a rough situation for him. He stated he misses the church and said, "One day I'm going to drive down to see you guys again." I asked him to stay in touch and keep my number. I told him I looked forward to seeing him soon.

We must not to burn every bridge which can be crossed in the future. In my ministry as a volunteer Jail Chaplain, I hear countless stories from prisoners inside the county jail. They tell me how many times they wished they could do it over again. They burned bridges with their families and are now regretting their mistakes. We never know what God will do when men like this decide to follow the leadership of Jesus Christ in the future. God's people everywhere depend upon us. We must understand the great power the Holy Spirit has to deal with people even outside the influence of the church. That's amazing love we can't always understand; and that's why He's God and we aren't.

The Person's Nonverbal Communicators

While conscious of your own behavior, it is obvious for me to mention the *person* you are interacting. All of the following areas listed will take into consideration established baseline. I would like to suggest a few cues which might be noteworthy:

1. The Facial Area - Since not all people are alike, understand that people are not all the same in how they respond to interaction. Each person will be different in interaction and as a result interpretations will be different. This is why it is important for us to spend *time* with them. Every person is different. We can't assume one cookie cutter approach to everyone, otherwise it will certainly backfire. In fact the differences might be seen even in reactions with differing people's makeups:

   > "... Findings may be interpreted as meaning that low empathic people react emotionally differently or even in a contradictory way compared to high empathic persons. It is therefore interesting to note that Laird proposed that there are individual differences that make some people more susceptible to facial feedback than others."[123]

The understanding of personalities is also important so you may be able to discern a significant change in behavior. This involves interacting with one personality type to another. Since one person may provide insignificant feedback during an interaction and when the behavior changes significantly, be aware of the changes. This way you can address that particular area in the coming minutes. Since personalities are so significant; understand people as much as you can before the interaction. Again, this takes *time*. If the person's facial expressions are fairly consistent throughout baseline, you may discern the person is being transparent.

---

[123] Per Andre'asson and Ulf Dimberg, *Emotional Empathy and Facial Feedback*, J Nonverbal Behavior (2008): 32:223.

This is good ground for the interaction. It will also allow you to engage in an honest conversation.

Smiles as stated before can be deceiving at times. These may be faked or produced at the person's desire. Some are even exhibited by nervousness and fear. Because of these difficulties, all nonverbal actions and cues are needed to determine the validity of the message (as many times repeated again). Remember too, that eyebrow feedback stays fairly consistent with most people and should be considered in baseline behavior. Most eyebrow raises and smiles are generated with the same muscles. Karen Schmidt, Sharika Bhattacharya and Rachel Denlinger state;

> "Comparing spontaneous smiles and eyebrow raises allows us to consider the differences in two facial displays commonly observed in social interactions. Because both are socially oriented facial displays, it is possible that both will exhibit similar movement characteristics."[124]

Since many of the indicators are varied in nature through observation and close examination to determine their congruency, normally you don't need to worry how these changes in each person are differed. This is somewhat comforting at this point since you have much to gather in the realm of determining the sender's intentions. If you try too much observation at one time, you won't actively listen. Try to keep the observation simple and not overcomplicate it.

Although the eyes also have much to determine the interactional level, eyes can suddenly begin moving side to side. This occurs suddenly when a person is either thinking about what to say or trying to orient the mind for a possible deceptive answer. In the realm of the eye, take the time to determine the behavior of the eye movement and then look for noticeable changes or deviations. One notable change could include the eyes rapidly moving back and forth horizontally. This might indicate a processing of

---

[124] Karen L. Schmidt, Sharika Bhattacharya, and Rachel Denlinger, *Comparison of Deliberate and Spontaneous Facial Movement in Smiles and Eyebrow Raises*, J Nonverbal Behavior (2009): 33:36.

information or processing the beginning of a lie. This can also be noted when other indicators such as body movement away from you begins or arms and legs begin to cross. They may be beginning to build a barrier of safety between you. These behavioral changes you must respond to in the coming minutes. Another area that is important is when the person will no longer maintain eye contact and lower the head to avoid eye contact. This action could signal shame. The head has now lowered to a point of submission or embarrassment. Since the facial area is where most feedback is observed, be aware of changes within the face and other signals which are congruent.

2. Body Posturing - Since baseline is now established, watch for signs of change within the behavior of the individual when certain points of the discussion lead to stressful or difficult situations. Recognition of these differences and the cues can help determine what the problem is. While they are seated you may notice the person distancing themselves. This could be sliding back their chair to provide space in times of stress. This change is different than the time where the person was leaning forward in the beginning. This can also be noted in times of standing while in the interaction process. When normal distancing is present, take note of the behavioral spacial change and seek to work through what is causing their intentional or unintentional distancing. Being aware of the change in behavior and acting immediately will extend our willingness (or biblical soberness) to help the person. This *soberness* is the willingness to convey passion to help the person. For instance, if a person who has begun the conversation with arms folded, note the behavior in baseline and determine this action may not necessarily be a negative action. It could merely be a comfortable position for the person. I know it is for me many times. Another instance could involve a person who is quite comfortable sitting with their legs crossed at the knee area causing an appearance of intentional distancing when in fact the action is merely a comfortable sitting position for the person or modesty for a woman. When you can identify these areas, it can lead

to signals of *meshing*. So what would be some good signs of the person *meshing* with the pastor?

Good indications of meshing would be:

   a. A person who slides slightly closer to the pastor in the interaction.

   b. A person who begins *mirroring* the behavior of the pastor by positioning his body to "mirror" his.

   c. A person who decreases their personal space over the time of the interaction.

   d. A person who might touch the pastor over the course of the interaction. Keep in mind some might try to convince you while lying by trying to use touch to convince you. Again, use multiple identifiers to confirm behavior.

So what might be some areas where problems might be noticed in spatial invasion? Martin Remland discusses a few that you might see when the conversation gets tough for them:

> "Most of the time, the victim of a spatial invasion will become uncomfortable and try to compensate in some way by backing up, turning to one side, reducing eye contact, or changing the topic of the conversation (if it were personal)."[125]

3. Touch - This area can be used at times which encourage positive behavior reinforcement when used by you. The simple touch of a person might reinforce their support or agreement during an interaction. When a person can pat you on the back, it helps you understand that meshing has begun and is a good sign of successful interaction. When a person takes your hand in tough times during an interaction, they may be signaling need for support. In fact during times of crisis, this may be the only contact which is needed to convey care.

---

[125] Remland, *Nonverbal Communication in Everyday Life*, 155.

4. Hand Gestures - The use of hand gestures is important as we saw in the last section. The use of hands is often used to communicate nonverbally in ways the verbal cannot express. Try to understand each one you see. If the signals are misunderstood, ask the person to connect the meaning of the hand gesture. The common usages of hand signals are important in every culture and need to be observed to determine clear understanding to the person's intentions. In other cases the use of hand gestures can signal incongruent behavior or trouble as stated by Calero:

    > "As an educated observer, you should look for the 'too many' gestures. Specifically, look for incongruent signs that contradict what on the surface appears to be confidence."[126]

5. Tightening Appearances and Stress - When times of stress affect the body, people will exhibit differing physical tightening's in the body. Some of these characteristics can be seen in the facial area such as teeth clinching, mouth area drawing upward with lips clenched together, noticeable wrinkling of the forehead, etc. In the body area several other changes can be noted by the hands, and fingers which are tightly interlocked. Other times people will hide their hands which were originally on the table and now hidden. Ankles sometimes will be viewed as locked; and finally, tightening of the torso area which affects their breathing. In the areas of stress, the person may exhibit sweat which was not formally a problem in the onset of the interaction. Then over time, the hands may feel sweaty when you shake hands to leave. Signs like this may also signal increased heart rate.

6. Signs of Incongruence - Henry Calero also points out a few interesting things which appear when what is being said does not line up with the rest of the body. He starts with this question:

---

[126] Calero, *The Power of Nonverbal Communication*, 81.

"What should you look for? What are 'the tells' of someone is making a 'tell?'"

He goes on to say how interrogators determine incongruences;

"Interrogators often simplify their jobs by looking for quick and simple cues that suggest incongruence in the people they interview. These cues include: Saying yes while you shake your head no; saying that you're not in a rush while you look at the clock; saying you don't mind being interviewed while frowning; saying you're not upset while speaking in one-word grunts."[127]

The important thing to understand is that incongruence is not necessarily a sign of lying. People are often nervous, inattentive to their actions or trying to hide something which is personal throughout the interaction. It is therefore important to observe these signs and try to let the person know they are in a safe environment. When the person is comfortable and settled they can now interact in a healthy way, which is the ultimate goal in the interaction.

After the Interaction

The importance of our growth in nonverbal communication cannot be understated. We are to be the best we can be for the Lord (Luke 12:48). For you to become the best you can be for the Lord, demands a follow up from you for those previously interacted. If you sense any unclear actions during the previous interaction which might cause future misunderstandings between you and the person, try to resolve anything. This is for the purpose of what might have been misperceived or misunderstood. It might even involve a second interaction to clear any unresolved issues or misunderstandings which might still be present as well. One of the ways you can avoid these kinds of repetitive meetings

---

[127] Ibid, 97.

can be through summarizing the interaction at its conclusion by asking some questions. It also allows more time for the two to get to know each other a little more by a second or repeated interaction. This is also where additional nonverbal cues for baseline behavior can be noted for the future. This is normally because the longer you talk, the more the person will return to their baseline behavior. This gives you more information to determine if your conclusion from the beginning is in sync with the time before.

Then after the interaction(s) are complete, you might begin to ask yourself a few questions regarding the interaction to see if you were effective. A few of these follow up areas are suggested by Lawrence Brammer and Ginger MacDonald by using the following guidelines:

1. *Attend* to the various *themes* and emotional *overtones* as helpees speak.
2. Put together the key ideas and feelings into *broad statements* of their basic meanings.
3. *Do not add* new ideas to your summary.
4. Decide if it would be more helpful to state your summary or ask them to summarize the basic themes, agreements, or plans. In deciding, consider your purpose:

   Was it to *warm up* helpees at the beginning of the interview?
   Was it to *focus* their scattered thoughts and feelings?
   Was it to *close* discussion on this theme?
   Was it to *check* your understanding of the interview progress?
   Was it to *encourage* them to explore themes more completely?
   Was it to *terminate* the relationship with a progress summary?
   Was it to *assure* them that their interviews were moving along well?[128]

To ask questions of ourselves in the end will also allow you to become a better communicator in the nonverbal realm. These questions although

---

[128] Brammer, Lawrence M., and Ginger MacDonald, *The Helping Relationship: Process and Skills* (Needham Heights, MA: Allyn and Bacon, 1999), 96.

verbally mentioned, may help to reinforce whether the nonverbal signals are being perceived and received correctly. This continues to keep you growing through the *novice* stage and on to true maturity or *good report*.

You also should be willing to take a look at the interactional process and try to determine where you might have better communicated with people. To do so, look at the closing minutes of the interaction to determine the receptivity of the person to the interaction. Were they under less fear or uncertainty than before the interaction? This will help mirror your read of the person and if it was accurate. Your success will be accomplished by meeting the requirements of scripture previously mentioned to determine if the characteristics were just the part of a calling to ministry or part of your everyday life. If you can look back at these qualifications and know you have met each, you can have a certainty of God's blessings on the interaction. When this is accomplished, you obtained the desired goal from the beginning. It will also affirm a good baseline condition for the person in the next interaction. More importantly it will allow the person to see the scriptural *good report* in your life and verify any misunderstandings which might have existed from the past. This self-evaluation process will allow you to determine if the interaction achieved its maximum effectiveness for the glory of God.

CHAPTER TEN
So Will This All Work?

Since this book involves real-life pastors who were questioned about nonverbal communication, mostly through electronic surveys, the concerns each one has about nonverbal communication nevertheless are real. You may want to test my research by developing a workshop in which this research can be studied in the real world with real people in a ministry setting. This type of "hands on" approach will allow you to determine your own effectiveness of my assertions throughout this book. This will also allow you to put the practices from this study into a real life environment to assist you in becoming a better communicator.

You might also ask why I consistently repeated myself throughout this book. The purpose of these reiterations was to reinforce the process and learning of nonverbal communication. It was not to insult your intelligence, but to reinforce previous learning. I always heard from college professors in the past that if you reiterate something three times, it becomes memory (or at least that's what they said). So I hope you won't take it this way.

The thing I do know is this: the information I developed through my studies, quoted experts in the field, and have applied theory and practice, has helped me to become a better communicator. I'll be honest with you though; it didn't occur overnight. Not only is this study practical to ministry, but has helped me to *connect* with people instead of merely *communicating* with them. Because of these practices and application over time, I have experienced a high success rate with people within ministry and counseling situations. To help you understand the relevance of my concern in nonverbal communication, I would like to share a few stories which might help illustrate the successes of how nonverbal communication can be observed and interacted so that people can receive the care they need.

For example, I encountered a young man who was literally ready to take his own life, but afraid to do so at the time. The young man had invested his entire soul in what he thought would be a lifelong relationship with a girl who broke up with him suddenly one night. His entire world fell apart and crashed from his point of view. He lost his will to live as result of his deep heartache. The occasion in which I encountered him was the result of a call for police service. This occurred while I was a law enforcement officer in a patrol officer capacity. The call for service was reported as a suspicious person underneath an inter-coastal bridge at two o'clock in the morning. This bridge was near a private housing area. It was really dark under the bridge that early morning. As I approached the bottom of the bridge area the man hid behind a structural support in the bridge, partially hiding himself from full view. I wasn't sure why he was hiding behind the pillar but keenly aware of potential danger as a police officer. At two o'clock in the morning under a dark bridge. After being asked to plainly show himself, the young man appeared from the shadows with one hand behind his back. Repeated attempts to convince the man to reveal his hands were unsuccessful. I noticed he was attempting to hide or concealing something (a potential threat). After realizing the intentional spacial distance created by the man and the young man to portray a potential threat, I took the time to communicate and leave the distance at approximately 30 feet. Observing his nonverbal language (by the use of a single hand gesture expressing frustration and dismay) at this time made a huge potential safety impact to me and possibly the young man. Over the next few minutes I was able to convey compassion and care nonverbally by using hand gestures. I was able to downgrade a somewhat tactical stance (while still remaining at a safe distance with cover immediately ready) which seemed to begin to de-escalate the situation. Over the next few minutes of initially establishing trust by letting him know I was there to help, the young man took his hand from behind his back. No weapon was viewed. When I saw his hand had no weapon, I calmly reassured the young man while slowly increasing spatial distance. This distance was previously established to a distance of 30 feet to now of less than five. Several minutes later the young man confided in me to explain his dilemma. He explained he was too afraid to take his own life, but thought if an officer saw his stance and potential weapon he might shoot him in self-defense.

He said this would produce an end to his pain; at least in his eyes. As a result of the entire incident, I was not only able to determine his nonverbal cues and attempt to increase initial trust, but communicate nonverbally in an effective way. I later led this young man to Christ on the tailgate of his pickup truck. The effect of distance decreased over the progression of the interaction, which initially allowed the safety of both parties in the interim. The frustration conveyed by the hands and facial expressions (congruent behavior) only expressed his grief instead of aggression. These identifiers would have not been properly understood without the aspect of time spent with him, along with observing other nonverbal indicators which reinforced the behavior. This information was taken by many additional indicators as well, which were exhibited by the young man. If I took one indicator taken at face value, the young man's actions could have produced some life altering consequences, including the possibility of his death. That might have been the result he was seeking, but the deeper and inner part of his soul was crying out for help. We as pastors are that life-line for those who are in need of help. Think of it this way: meeting a perceived threat from 30 feet away, to sitting on a tailgate of a truck talking like old friends; then leading your new friend to Christ. What a wonderful God we serve.

In the realm of nonverbal communication with fellow believers, God has given believers the ability to recognize nonverbal behavior with additional insight from the Holy Spirit. It's called discernment, but it doesn't occur overnight. This is important since there is a common spirit within the interaction. When dealing with Christians, you must understand the Holy Spirit has insight into the core of the fellow believer, like nothing we could ever gain. If you want to *connect* with the person, you go to the One who knows the person's core. This involves discernment prior to the interaction by way of prayer for the soul in need. We begin asking God for discernment. Then God allows the person to unzip their heart to someone who wants to care for them. When the core is affected over time by influences of sinful man and world, an outward manifestation is clearly seen by the Holy Spirit. This insight into the core of the believer can be discerned by the Holy Spirit's presence within the pastor. It's available. As I have said it before, no one knows man better than God.

Second Story: In ministry experience, I experienced another encounter with an 18 year old Christian man who recently lost a lifelong Christian mentor. This older mentor had a great level of influence on the young man's life. One evening I received a disparaging call from the young man. The young man asked if he could meet with me immediately at his home on the other side of town. After agreeing to meet him, I drove across town praying along the way asking for insight. When I arrived at his house, he appeared a few minutes later at the front door. The young man came to the door with his shoulders hanging really low (normally completely upright with plenty of energy), his head lowered (no longer revealing his great smile), and a really sluggish movement (instead of jumping off the front porch as usual). This was an unusually quiet demeanor for his normal behavior. As I watched the behavior, I knew there was a great change in his behavior from his previous baseline norms. His demeanor revealed a devastated emotional condition by something which occurred within the last few hours. He had red eyes, dried tears, and the look of complete anguish on his face. His facial and body behavior had changed so significantly from other times of encountering him it was obvious that something very bad had happened. The nonverbal indicators I heard were also a groaning within the soul of the young man by his heavy sighs at times. After talking for a few minutes inside his home, the young man asked me if we could take a drive to his friend's house. While driving to the location, I began to pray for discernment and wisdom on how to respond. At this time he was no obvious threat in any capacity. He didn't have much energy to even move around. After arriving at a house a few blocks away from my home, the young man got out of my car and walked around the back side of the house. I got out and followed him. After looking in the back sliding glass door a piece of rope was still hanging from the ceiling. This is where his mentor who had such an influence on his life ended his own. The young man replied, "There is a lot of pain in this house." Within my spirit, a voice came forward which said, "The pain is not in this house." "It's in him." Several months of counsel occurred before this young man was able to trust or allow people to invest in him. We spent a lot of time together. That person later became me. To this day, this young man (who is now in his late thirties) has three small children and raising a family. Although he is not particularly active in the church today, he still seeks me out when I enter the business where he is a manager of a restaurant. We all communicate, but not all connect. Connections in life are not only part of our calling but requirements to lasting relationships.

The assessment of potential violence can be determined within a short time in some encounters (like the first story) and spacial distance gives you some time. This time is what you need to become aware of your surroundings and time to react if the need occurs. Note how I used distance while taking time to develop initial rapport, whether known or unknown. With the acts of violence every increasing in our world today, we should be wiser than ever when potential danger could or might occur. Distance is your friend in these cases. As you pray and ask for discernment, make sure the voice you hear is that of God and not your personal desire to interact with people who might be of personal danger to you. When the hair stands up on the back of your neck, don't be afraid to listen to it either. I have over the course of twenty-five years and it saved my skin many times.

Some Closing Thoughts

Because this study is limited to North American societal norms of behavior, we must be careful when trying to interact with people outside the continental United States using these methods. Since many of us travel abroad to do conduct mission work in foreign countries, I caution the use of these facts and findings in such areas. This is due to cultural and communicational differences within respective countries. To use this study's conclusions in foreign countries may create problems, frustrations, and misunderstandings in communication for each side of the interaction. The process might become more effective in these foreign nations if there is enough time to study, and understand the cultural norms of society. Then you might begin to implement them very slowly. This would take a large amount of time to do so though, so take your time so you won't make irreversible mistakes.

When you can culminate the basic knowledge of nonverbal communication skills, and biblical mandate of scripture covered in 1 Timothy 3 into your life, you will become a pastor which is able to effectively communicate with people in a way which honors God in his service. By your understanding of the nonverbal communication process, you will be able to understand people at a deeper level. This deeper relationship with people will help to lead them to a life which is to ultimately glorify God. These relationships will also become memories shared by each of you for the glory of our Lord and Savior Jesus Christ.

When people sense your commitment to their lives and care, the relationship can move on to greater heights as the entire body of Christ glorifies God. This is the calling of you to His people. And it begins with one life at a time. The first question of the Westminster Catechism states, "What is the chief end of man?" The answer to this question is, "Man's chief end is to glorify God." Help them to do that and I pray the Lord Jesus Christ uses you in wonderful ways for His Kingdom!

E. M. Griffin gives us these final words concluding our study together:

> "Nonverbal communication is the punctuation that tells
> us how to interpret words; thus it is the final arbiter of our
> relationships."[129]

Good lasting relationships are of quality, not quantity. Jesus took three plus years with only 12 and look what happened to the world!

---

[129] Griffin, *Making Friends and Making Them Count*, 117.

BIBLIOGRAPHY

Ambadar, Zara, Jeffrey F. Cohn, and Lawrence Ian Reed. "All Smiles are Not Created Equal: Morphology and Timing of Smiles Perceived as Amused, Polite, and Embarrassed/Nervous." *J Nonverbal Behavior 33* (2009): 17–34.

Andre'asson, Per, and Ulf Dimberg. "Emotional Empathy and Facial Feedback." *J Nonverbal Behavior 32* (2008): 215–224.

Boyd, Gregory A., and Paul R. Eddy. *Across the Spectrum: Understanding Issues in Evangelical Theology.* Grand Rapids, MI: Baker Academic, 2007.

Brammer, Lawrence M., and Ginger MacDonald. *The Helping Relationship: Process and Skills.* Needham Heights, MA: Allyn and Bacon, 1999.

Burgoon, Judee K., Laura A. Guerrero, and Kory Floyd. *Nonverbal Communication.* Boston, MA: Pearson Education Inc., 2010.

Burley-Allen, Madelyn. *Listening, The Forgotten Skill: A Self Teaching Guide.* New York, NY: John Wiley & Sons, Inc., 1995.

Calero, Henry. *The Power of Nonverbal Communication: How You Act is More Important than What You Say.* Aberdeen WA: Silver Lake Publishing, 2005.

Cesario, Joseph and Tory E. Higgins. "Making Message Recipients 'Feel Right': How Nonverbal Cues Can Increase Persuasion." *Association for Psychological Science Vol. 19, Number 5* (2008): 415-420.

Chambers, Oswald. *Conformed to His Image: The Servant as His Lord: Lessons on Living Like Jesus*. Grand Rapids, MI: Discovery House Publishers, 1996.

Crabb, Larry. *Connecting: Healing for Ourselves and our Relationships*. Nashville, TN: Thomas Nelson, 2005.

Dolinski, Dariusz. "Touch, Compliance, and Homophobia." *J Nonverbal Behavior 34* (2010):179–192.

Florida Department of Law Enforcement. "Investigative Interviews, Advanced Course #047." Tallahassee, FL: Criminal Justice Standards and Training Commission, 1989.

Forgas, Joseph P., and Rebekah East. "How real is that Smile? Mood Effects on Accepting or Rejecting the Veracity of Emotional Facial Expressions." *J Nonverbal Behavior 32* (2008):157–170.

Foster, Kenneth Neill. "Discernment, the powers and spirit speaking," Doctor of Phil. diss., Fuller Theological Seminary, 1988. In ProQuest. http://proquest.umi.com.ezproxy.liberty.edu:2048/pqdlink?Ver=1&Exp=11-07-2016&FMT=7&DID=743957101&RQT=309&attempt=1 (accessed November 8, 2011).

Goman, Carol Kinsey. "Watch Your Language." *America Society for Training and Development* (August 2008): 94-95.

Gore, Jonathan S. "The Interaction of Sex, Verbal, and Nonverbal Cues in Same-Sex First Encounters." *J Nonverbal Behavior 33* (2009): 279–299.

Griffin, EM. *Making Friends and Making Them Count*. Downer Grove, IL: Inter Varsity Press, 1987.

Harney, Kevin. *Leadership from the Inside Out: Examining the Inner Life of a Healthy Church Leader*. Grand Rapids, MI: Zondervan, 2007.

Hawkins, Ron. "COUN 852: Growth and Development of the Contemporary Minister." (Lecture, Liberty Theological Seminary, May 24, 2011).

Hofmann, Wilhelm, Tobias Gschwendner, and Manfred Schmitt. "The Road to the Unconscious Self Not Taken: Discrepancies between Self and Observer-Inferences about Implicit Dispositions from Nonverbal Behavioral Cues." *European Journal of Personality 23* (2009): 343-366.

Jagnow, Dieter Joel. "Communication Principles in Pastoral Counseling," Master thesis, Concordia Seminary, 1993. In TREN. http://www.tren. com.ezproxy.liberty.edu:2048/e-docs/search.cfm (accessed November 7, 2011).

Jones, Susanne M., and John G. Wirtz. "Sad Monkey See, Monkey Do: Nonverbal Matching in Emotional Support Encounters." *Communication Studies Vol. 58, No. 1* (March 2007): 71-86.

Kahn, Carolyn J. "Non-Verbal Communications: A Review of the Theories and its Applicability to Guidance and Counseling," Master of Science thesis, Southern Connecticut State College, 1968. In ProQuest. http://rx9vh3hy4r.search.serialssolutions. com/?ctx_ver=Z39.88-2004&ctx_enc=info%3Aofi%2Fenc%3AUTF-8&rfr_id=info:sid/summon.serialssolutions.com&rft_val_fmt=info:ofi/fmt:kev:mtx:dissertation&rft.genre=dissertation&rft.title=Non-verbal+c ommunications%3A+A+review+of+the+theories+and+its+applicability+to+guidance+and+counseling&rft.DBID=C16;DMQ;DMR;KFU;KFT&rft. PQPubID=EP28152&rft.au=Kahn%2C+Carolyn+J&rft.date=1968-12-31&rft.externalDBID=n%2Fa&rft.externalDocID=1955580331 (accessed November 8, 2011).

Kendon, Adam. "Spacing and Orientation in Co-present Interaction." *Lecture Notes in Computer Science, Volume 5967, Development of Multimodal Interfaces: Active Listening and Synchrony* (2010): 1-15.

Knapp, Mark L., and Judith A. Hall. *Nonverbal Communication in Human Interaction*. Boston, MA: Wadsworth Cengage Learning, 2010.

Krumhuber, Eva, Antony Manstead S. R., and Arvid Kappas. "Temporal Aspects of Facial Displays in Person and Expression Perception: The Effects of Smile Dynamics, Head-Tilt, and Gender." *J Nonverbal Behavior 31* (2007): 39–56.

Kulp, John. "Developing Empathy and Intimacy through Communication," DMin. diss., Denver Conservative Baptist Seminary, 2003. In TREN. http://www.tren.com.ezproxy.liberty.edu:2048/e-docs/search.cfm?p090-0298 (accessed November 7, 2011).

Leal, Sharon, and Aldert Vrij. "Blinking During and after Lying." *J Nonverbal Behavior 32* (2008): 187-194.

Ludwick, Sabina. "The Grace of God in Biblical Counseling," Master thesis, The Master's College, 2007. In TREN. http://www.tren.com.ezproxy.liberty.edu:2048/e-docs/download2.cfm (accessed February, 28, 2012).

Maxwell, John C. *Everyone Communicates, Few Connect: What the Most Effective People do Differently*. Nashville, TN: Thomas Nelson Inc., 2010.

McMillan, David O. "The Development and Use of the McMillan Affective Relationship Scale in Measuring the Effects of Verbal Interaction and of Selected Non-Verbal Techniques of Communication on Synthesized Desirable Outcomes of Group Dynamics Procedures in Sensitivity Training," Doctor of Phil. diss., East Texas State University, 1971. In ProQuest. http://rx9vh3hy4r.search.serialssolutions.com/?ctx_ver=Z39.88-2004&ctx_enc=info%3Aofi%2Fenc%3AUTF-8&rfr_id=info:sid/summon.serialssolutions.com&rft_val_fmt=info:ofi/fmt:kev:mtx:dissertation&rft.genre=dissertation&rft.title=THE+DEVELOP-MENT+AND+USE+OF+THE+MC+MILLAN+AFFECTIVE+RELA-

TIONSHIP+SCALE+IN+MEASURING+THE+EFFECTS+OF+VER-
BAL+INTERACTION+AND+OF+SELECTED+NON-VE-
RBAL+TECHNIQUES+OF+COMMUNICATION+ON+SYN-
THESIZED+DESIRABLE+OUTCOMES+OF+GROUP+DY-
NAMICS+PROCEDURES+IN+SENSITIVITY+TRAINING&rft.
DBID=C16;DMQ;DMR;KFU;KFT&rft.PQPubID=7210802&rft.
au=MC+MILLAN%2C+O.+DAVID&rft.date=1971-09-01&rft.exter-
nalDBID=n%2Fa&rft.externalDocID=757620721 (accessed November
8, 2011).

Navarro, Joe. Louder than Words: *Take your Career from Average to
Exceptional with the Hidden Power of Nonverbal Intelligence.* New York,
NY: HarperCollins Publishers, 2009.

Neff, Blake. *A Pastors Guide to Interpersonal Communication: The Other Six
Days.* Binghamton, NY, Haworth Pastoral Press, 2006.

Ortberg, John. *The Me I Want to Be: Becoming God's Best Version of You.*
Grand Rapids, MI: Zondervan, 2010.

Oswald, Roy M. *Clergy Self Care: Finding a Balance for Effective Ministry.*
New York, NY: Alban Institute, 1993.

Peters, Pamela. "Gaining Compliance through Non-Verbal
Communication." *Pepperdine Dispute Resolution Law Journal 87*
(2007): 112.

Practicing Pastoral Counseling in the United Methodist Mode. *Quarterly
Review: A Journal of Theological Resources for Ministry, Vol. 25* (Winter
2005): 337-435.

Remland, Martin. *Nonverbal Communication in Everyday Life.* Boston.
MA: Houghton Mifflin Company, 2003.

Robertson, A. T. *Word Pictures in the New Testament*. Nashville, TN: Broadman Press, 1930.

Salovey, Peter, and John D. Mayer. "Emotional Intelligence" Imagination, Cognition and Personality." *Imagination, Cognition and Personality, Vol. 9-3* (1989-1990): 185-211.

Scazzero, Peter, and Warren Bird. *The Emotionally Healthy Church: A Strategy for Discipleship that Actually Changes Lives*. Grand Rapids, MI: Zondervan, 2003.

Schmidt, Karen L., Sharika Bhattacharya, and Rachel Denlinger. "Comparison of Deliberate and Spontaneous Facial Movement in Smiles and Eyebrow Raises." *J Nonverbal Behavior 33* (2009): 35–45.

Smith, Fraser W., and Philippe G. Schyns, "Smile Through Your Fear and Sadness Transmitting and Identifying Facial Expression Signals Over a Range of Viewing Distances." *Psychology Science, Volume 20* (November 10, 2009): 1202-1208.

Smith, Fred. "How to Be Heard." *Your Church* (September/ October 2007): 104.

Stanley, Charles. *How to Handle Adversity*. Nashville, TN: Oliver-Nelson Books, 1989.

Swenson, Richard A. *Margin: Restoring Emotional, Physical, Financial and Time Reserves to Overloaded Lives*. Colorado Springs, CO: NavPress, 2004.

Swift, John. "Toward a Theoretical and Theological Framework for the use of Therapeutic Non-Verbal Communication Experiences in Group Pastoral Counseling," DMin. thesis, School of Theology at Claremount, 1969. In ProQuest. http://rx9vh3hy4r.search.serialssolutions. com/?ctx_ver=Z39.88-2004&ctx_enc=info%3Aofi%2Fenc%3AUTF-8&rfr_id=info:sid/summon.serialssolutions.com&rft_val_fmt=info:ofi/

fmt:kev:mtx:dissertation&rft.genre=dissertation&rft.title=Toward+a+the oretical+and+theological+framework+for+the+use+of+therapeutic+non-ve rbal+communication+experiences+in+group+pastoral+counseling&rft. DBID=C16;DMQ;DMR;KFU;KFT&rft.PQPubID=DP11625&rft. au=Swift%2C+John+K&rft.date=1969-07-01&rft.isbn=0496107003&rft. externalDBID=n%2Fa&rft.externalDocID=813831801   (accessed November 8, 2011).

Thompson, George J., and Jerry Jenkins. *Verbal Judo: The Gentle Art of Persuasion*. New York, NY: William Morrow and Company Inc., 1993.

Towns, Elmer. *Understanding the Deeper Life: A Guide to Christian Experience*. Old Tappen, NJ: Fleming H. Revel Company, 1988.

Walters, Stan B. *Practical Kinesic Interview and Interrogation: Level 1 and 2 Course*. Indianapolis, IN: Stan Walter and Associates, 2009.

Warren, Gemma, Elizabeth Schertler, and Peter Bull. "Detecting Deception from Emotional and Unemotional Cues." *J Nonverbal Behavior 33* (2008): 59-69.

Wilson, Michael Todd, and Brad Hoffman. *Preventing Ministry Failure: A Shepherd Care Guide for Pastors, Ministers and Other Caregivers*. Downer Grove, IL: Inter Varsity Press, 2007.

Webster's Dictionary Online. http://dictionary.reference.com/browse/ circumspect, (accessed December 4, 2011).

Young's Analytical Concordance of the Bible. Peabody, MA: Hendrickson Publishers, 2005.

Printed in the United States
By Bookmasters